Quality Assurance in Libraries Series 1

A textbook on

QUALITY MANAGEMENT IN LIBRARIES

Quality Assurance in Libraries Series 1

A textbook on QUALITY MANAGEMENT IN LIBRARIES

Sneha Tripathi
Assistant Librarian
Sayaji Rao Gaekwad Library
Banaras Hindu University

Aditya Tripathi
Assistant Professor
Department of Library and Information Science
Banaras Hindu University

Ess Ess Publications
New Delhi

Quality Assurance in Libraries Series 1
A Testbook on
Quality Management in Libraries

ISBN: 978-81-7000-808-8

First Published 2016

Published by:
Ess Ess Publications
4831/24, Ansari Road,
Darya Ganj,
New Delhi-110 002.
INDIA
Phones: 23260807, 41563444
Fax: 41563334
E-mail: info@essessreference.com
www.essessreference.com

Cover Design by *Patch Creative Unit*

Printed and bound in India at Salasar Imaging Systems.

CONTENTS

PREFACE

When the human's initial quest for survival was settled, they realized the need to have a quality life. This is evident through the remains of earlier civilizations such as Mesopotamian, Egyptian, Indian, and Chinese and the continuous transition of the society from pre-agricultural to agrarian, then to industrial and now the existing information age. The meaning and standards for "quality" have been changing (or we can say improving), once the target was achieved. Thus, "quality" is a never-ending, continuum process which is essential for the development of the society.

Today, every organization, profit or non-profit, is working to meet the guidelines and standards to qualify their products/services as "quality" by the society. Libraries are no-exception to it. They work to satisfy the information needs of their users at the right time. For this, they have to devise new services through exploitation of information and communication technological tools, evaluate their services and renew their services based on user's feedback. These all are some specifications which a library can use to provide services that could be tagged as "quality" by their users. A library failing to do so may lose their existing users, will have rare chances to attract their potential users and the parent organization would not like to fund for library services.

It seems important, then, the library professionals

and administrators should be aware of the concept "Quality" and "Total Quality Management" as well as the international standards available. The present work is developed primarily as a textbook for B.L.I.Sc. and M.L.I.Sc. courses. A serious attempt has been made to include all important views of the stalwarts from the field of Quality Management. The concentration is primarily on to explain the various aspects of Quality and Total Quality Management from the perspective of a library professional. It characterizes a Quality System for libraries based on ISO 9001, an international standard for quality assurance system, for the libraries. This is to be noted here that the proposed quality management system for libraries is based on ISO 9001:1994. ISO 9001:1994 along with ISO 9002:1994 and ISO 9003:1994 became obsolete as soon as ISO 9001:2000 came into existence. In ISO 9001:2000, ISO has abandoned the 20-clause structure of the old standard. Instead of 20 sections, the new standard now has 5 sections under which these 20 clauses were reorganized. This was done to create a more logical structure and make it more compatible with ISO 14001 (a family of standards related to environmental management). ISO 9001:2000 addresses the issues related to customer requirements and satisfaction in much greater detail than ISO 9001:1994. It also emphasizes on the evaluation of the effectiveness and suitability of an organization's Quality management system and also the identification and implementation of systemic improvements. Both standards are elaborated and studied comprehensively under various headings of *Section 4.3*. Later on, ISO 9001:2008 was introduced which actually re-narrated the essence of ISO 9001:2000. It has only introduced clarifications to the existing requirements of ISO 9001:2000 and some changes intended to improve consistency with ISO 14001:2004. There were no new requirements. This is the current version of ISO standard. Since 2012, ISO 9001:2008 is under revision and is expected to be published in the end of 2015. Thus, the proposed Quality Management System which is mainly based on ISO 9001:1994 still holds relevant and can be applied to the libraries for ISO certification.

1
Introduction

Let us start with a scenario, where a library user approaches the reference desk of library A and library B with an urgent need to find 50 years of statistical data about rainfall recorded during rainy season in Cherrapunji, India. Out of library A and library B, the one which takes more time or unable to locate the correct source of information may lose that particular library user permanently or will have bleak chances to have that user again in their premise. Here, performance is judged against the yardstick of user satisfaction. Thus, an organizations performance, be it in the form of a service or product, is directly proportional to user satisfaction. If we see the scenario from an Organization's (in this case, library) perspective, they call it performance. However, the user may call it "Quality".

Being a service centered organization, libraries and information centers are vested with the responsibility to cater the needs and expectations of their library users. They collect information, store it and have the responsibility of disseminating the stored information to their respective users. Library services are modeled around their user's needs and expectations. And "users" always have expectation of quick, reliable efficient and round-the-clock services from the library, which leads one to the premises of the concept "quality". Quality is very well benchmarked in almost all sort of services like bank, railways, security, hospital, hotel etc. and in the products like automobiles, electronics, construction materials or consumables. Today, everyone in society talks of the term "Quality".

Generally "Quality" means, lower cost, high efficiency, high performance, high reliability and serviceability or in other words "Perfection". The other name which is coined to it is "Customer Satisfaction". For example- in a hospital if concerned doctors are available round the clock, nurses and staffs attend each patient at right time, and it is having all sorts of facilities then the patients are assured of quality medication. Attributes which determine the quality of "toothpaste" are- it should be tasty, can clean the teeth, good for gums, can strengthen the teeth and is able to protect the enamel, etc.

In other words, "Quality" is the viewpoint of the customer i.e. how far product suits him. For example, a company makes two types of utensils, one made up of clay and other made up of metal. The earlier one is lesser in cost than the latter one. If a customer comes and asks for a utensil which can store the water for one day, for him the earlier one will be the quality product because it satisfies all his needs at low cost irrespective of the fact that the latter is quite durable than the earlier one.

1.1. HISTORY OF QUALITY

The concept of quality has been inherent in the course of human evolution. Man's quest for better life has been evident through the remains of earlier civilizations (Drainage System of Indus Valley Civilization) and ruins of ancient cities (Pyramids by ancient Egyptians). The expedition is still on and amenities such as advanced medical treatments, improved education system, new modes of recreation and entertainment, development of information and communication technologies are the outcomes to improve the quality of life. These are testimonials for Quality, w hich existed in our skilled craftsmen, artisans, planners and engineers.

According to **R.M. Persig**:

"Quality is neither mind nor matter, but a third entity independent of the two... even though quality cannot be defined, you know what it is."

This particular approach defines quality as an abstract property. That means quality cannot be defined. A person can only experience it. This definition is basically borrowed from the viewpoint of Plato, where he argues that beauty can be only experienced it cannot be measured.

According to **L. Abbott**:

"Differences in quality amount to differences in quantity of some desired ingredient or attribute."

This viewpoint of the quality says that it is measurable but on the basis of certain variables which you can precisely measure. This particular definition of quality first appeared in the economics literature.

The latest view about the quality is nothing but the user-based approach. Different experts from the field of quality management have given several definitions for this particular approach.

According to **W. Edwards Deming**:

"Quality can be defined only in the terms of the agent. Who is the judge of the quality?

In the mind of the production worker, he produces quality if he can take pride in his work. Poor quality, to him means the loss of business, and perhaps his job. A good quality, he thinks, will keep the company in business. All this is as true in the service industries as it is in manufacturing."

J. M. Juran, initially defined Quality as "fitness for use": Later on, he amended his viewpoint and redefined it in terms of

a. Product features that meet customer needs, and

b. Freedom from deficiencies

The word quality also refers to freedom from deficiencies. Deficiencies may take various forms such as:

- Late deliveries
- Field failures
- Incorrect invoices
- Cancellation of sales contracts
- Factory scrap or rework
- Engineering design changes

Deficiency results in complaints, claims, returns, rework, and other damage. These collectively are forms of "product dissatisfaction" which ultimately brings "customer dissatisfaction."

Freedom from deficiencies can also be referred as "Quality of Conformance". It helps in reduction of variability and elimination of defects. Prevention and appraisal costs increases with the increase in level of Quality of conformance. Failure costs are expected to decrease as the level of Quality of conformance increases. Higher conformance leads to fewer complaints and increased customer satisfaction.

According to **Ishikawa**:

Quality is "satisfying the true requirements of the consumer".

According to, **Genichi Taguchi :**

"The ideal quality the customer can expect is

> *that every product delivers the target performance each time the product is used, under all intended operating conditions, and throughout its intended life, with no harmful side effects".*

Thus this view supports the customer's view on the quality that is:

> *"Customer satisfaction or Customer delight in the existing environment".*

Or

> *"Quality of a product (or service) is the customer's perception of the degree to which the product or service meets his or her expectations, in the existing environment."*

According to **Philip Crosby**:

It is "conformance to requirement".

This approach defines that the quality should be conformed according to the well-established norms and standards. These norms must be satisfied, if it is not, that means, the product in question is not a quality product. These specifications are based on the reduction of cost, just-in-time concept, and overall economy in the plant.

According to the '**Quality management and quality assurance- Vocabulary ISO 8402:1994**':

> *"Totality of characteristics of an entity that bear on its ability to satisfy stated and implied needs".*

According to **A. V. Feigenbaum** "Quality means best for certain customer conditions. These conditions are-

a. the actual use and

b. the selling price of the product

This definition actually defines the quality in terms of cost and prices. It says that quality product is one which provides performance at an acceptable price or in conformance to an acceptable cost. He further elaborates "Quality is the total composite product and service characteristics of marketing, engineering, manufacturing and maintenance through which the product and service in use will meet the expectations by the customer."

Feigenbaum is the originator of the concept "Total Quality Control" which later became popular as Total Quality Management.

1.2. WHY QUALITY IS REQUIRED

World War II necessitated the need of the tremendous amount of the production of artillery. Due to the increasing complexity of the products and services the idea of the quality started building up. The firms began to develop a separate decision making unit as well as operating framework for product quality, which was quite effective to take suitable action on the quality control findings. Particularly, some company in Japan felt the need of the quality improvement in their production. This idea crept in their mind because after the World War II Japanese were not competitive in the world market. During the same time Dr. Juran and Dr. Deming also taught them on Statistical Quality Control. Japanese firms had a common aim after 1950, i.e. Quality.

After 70's there was a shift in the very concept of business. It now shifted to **Buyer's market** from **Seller's market**. And the motto became Customer-satisfaction. Many top executives became quite serious about the product-quality. It required the effective leadership. This particular need was felt very much in the beginning of the 80's. In the late 80's the incorporation of the leadership has been done and a new concept of Total quality management came up.

Dr. Juran gave the concept of Big Q and Small Q in order to recognize the drastic shift between the period of before and after 80s. According to him, until 80s, the concept of quality was attached only to manufacturing firms and their products whose major objective was to make profit. The end users concern about the product was little relevant while designing of the product and relied only on the conformance to industry standards. The idea of quality was limited; hence, the name 'Small Q' is used. However, after 80s the concept got widespread and its significance in different sectors of the society including service sectors like libraries, which are purely not-for-profit organizations, was recognized. Feedback from customers/end users became highly relevant in the product design. The nature of the quality became more dynamic and comprehensive representing a big picture. The era represents 'Big Q'.

1.3. ABOUT "TOTAL QUALITY MANAGEMENT"

Before getting into the detail of Total Quality Management, it is worth understanding some basic terms that is involved in the whole process of TQM:

Product

A product is a thing that is offered for use to a target customer/user with the aim of allowing them to satisfy their needs and wants. A product

- helps them to achieve goals
- also helps them to solve a "problem"

A product can be:

a. Tangible like laptop, toothpaste, car, etc.

b. Intangible such as concepts, ideas, software, music, etc. Or

c. A mix of both such as, people, organizations, amusement parks, etc.

Product features have a remarkable impact on the profit, either monetary or in terms of user satisfaction (for organizations like libraries), of an organization. Product features are also referred as *Quality of Design*.

Increasing the Quality of the design generally leads to higher costs.

Customers

There are two distinct types of customers:

a. Internal Customers: Internal customers are from within the organization-the colleagues working together for delivering a service or product for the external customer.

b. External Customers: An external customer may be an individual or an enterprise that hires, purchases or make use of the product(s) or service(s) from another person or organization in exchange of money.

1.3.1. TQM

TQM is an umbrella methodology for continually improving the quality of all processes. According to Oakland, J. S. (1991)

> *"Total Quality Management (TQM) is an approach to improving the effectiveness and flexibility of business as a whole. It is essentially a way of organizing and involving the whole organization; every department, every activity, every single person at every level."*

TQM draws on knowledge of the principles and practices of [American Society for Quality]:

- the behavioral sciences
- the analysis of quantitative and non-quantitative data
- economic theories
- process analysis

The concept and philosophy evolved as a whole during 1980s [Angel R. Martínez Lorente, Frank Dewhurst, Barrie G. Dale, (1998)]. TQM added a new perspective to traditional organizational management and made it more flexible and approachable. Schmidt, W. and Finnigan, J. (1993) has drawn comparison between traditional and TQM based organizations (Table 1).

Table 1: Comparison between Traditional and TQM based Organizations

	Traditional	*TQM based Organization*
Structure	Hierarchical	Flatter, less hierarchical
Line of Authority	Rigid	Flexible
Strategy	Focus on maintaining Status-quo	Continuous Improvement
Relationship with Top Management	Strict vigilance from top management, Characterized by dependency, Fear and control	Characterized by Cordial, Interdependent, Trust and Mutual Understanding based
Relationship between employees	Focus on individual efforts, Competitiveness	Team efforts, Coordinated approach towards the goal
Managerial Perspective on staff and training	Burden, training as an additional cost to the organization	Staff as an asset and training as an investment
Quality Approach	Based on industrial standards set forth by management	Based on customer satisfaction
Decision Making	Based on intuition	Based on facts and feedback system

Total quality management involves three ideas in it.

- Total
- Quality
- Management

Total

It means 100 %. It can't be less than that. It calls for the participation of every individual in the organization in the quality maintenance process starting from top to bottom level. Ideally, it needs their full commitment for doing business. It not only involves all the employees of the firm but also the target customers of the organization is serving. They play major role in deciding the direction of the business. Their taste should be always kept in the consideration. If customer is satisfied that means the company is on the right track of the business.

Quality

According to the 'Quality management and quality assurance- Vocabulary ISO 8402:1994':

> *"Totality of characteristics of an entity that bear on its ability to satisfy stated and implied needs".*

UNESCO [Vlasceanu, L., Grunberg, L. and Parlea, D. (2007)] defines quality in the perspective of higher education as a multi-dimensional, multilevel, and dynamic concept that relates to the contextual settings of an educational model, to the institutional mission and objectives, as well as to specific standards within a given system, institution, programme, or discipline. According to them, quality may take different, sometimes conflicting, meanings depending on (i) the understanding of various interests of different constituencies or stakeholders in higher education (e.g. students; universities; disciplines; the labour market; society; a government); (ii) its references: inputs, processes, outputs, missions, objectives, etc.; (iii) the attributes or characteristics of the academic world worth evaluating; and (iv) the historical period in the development of higher education.

They have elaborated the concept of quality (for academic institutions) based on various existing for quality definitions :

a. Quality as excellence: a traditional, elitist academic view, according to which only the best standards of excellence (usually meaning a high level of difficulty and of complexity of a programme, the seriousness of the student testing procedures, etc.) are understood as true indicator of academic quality.

b. Quality as fitness for purpose: a concept that stresses the need to meet generally accepted standards such as those defined by an accreditation or quality assurance body, the focus being on the effectiveness of the processes at work in the institution or programme in fulfilling its objectives and mission. Sometimes quality in this sense is also labeled as: (i) a value for money approach owing to the (implicit) focus on how the inputs are effectively and efficiently used by the processes and mechanisms involved or (ii) the value-added approach when results are evaluated in terms of changes obtained through various educational processes (e.g. teaching and learning processes). A variation of the latter is the quality as transformation approach, which is strongly student-centered. It considers quality as a process of change, adding value to students through their learning experience.

c. Quality as fitness of purpose: a concept that focuses on the defined objectives and mission of the institution or programme with no check of the fitness of the processes themselves in regard to any external objectives or expectations. Fitness of purpose evaluates whether the quality related intention of an organization are adequate. Within this approach, one may distinguish alternative approaches developed in the 1990s: (i) quality as threshold whereby certain norms and criteria are set, which any programme or institution has to reach to be considered to be of quality. In many European higher education systems, a variant defining quality as a basic standard, closely linked to accreditation, is used. In this case, the starting point is the specification of a set of minimum standards to be met by an institution or programme and to generate the basis for the development of quality improvement mechanisms; (ii) quality as consumer satisfaction: quality perceived as closely linked to the growing importance of market forces in higher education, that focuses on the importance of the external expectations of consumers (students, families, society at large) and other stakeholders.

d. Quality as enhancement or improvement: focusing on the continuous search for permanent improvement, stressing the responsibility of the higher education institution to make the best use of its institutional autonomy and freedom. Achieving quality is central to the academic ethos and to the idea that academics themselves know best what quality is.

Each approach has advantages and disadvantages, being more or less suitable for a specific period of time or national context. In terms of evolution, there are permanent movement and oscillations between relative versus absolute, internal versus externally oriented, and basic versus more advanced and sophisticated notions of quality. However, common to all of these quality approaches is the integration of the following elements: (i) the guaranteed realization of minimal standards and benchmarks; (ii) the capacity to set the objectives in a diversifying context and to achieve them with the given input and context variables; (iii) the ability to satisfy the demands and expectations of direct and indirect consumers and stakeholders; (iv) the drive towards excellence.

Management

Management involves:

- Structures
- Systems
- Procedures
- Processes
- Continuous improvement

So, if we finally try to define the Total quality management:

> *"TQM is an integrated organizational effort in delighting customers (both external and internal) by meeting their expectations on a continuous basis through everyone involved with the organization working on continuous improvement in all products, services and processes along with the proper problem solving methodology."*

1.3.2. Elements of TQM

There are four basic elements of the TQM:

- People
- Appropriate technology
- Problem solving tools/ procedures
- Continuous improvement

1.3.3. Implementation of TQM

The implementation of TQM starts from the transformation of the old mind set to the new mind set.

- Changing the management and employee thought process
- Establishing a management system and process that reflects this new mind set
- Prompting and applying the tools in support of management

Broad elements in the TQM implementation are:

- Pilot projects and teams
- Leadership
- Organizational Structure
- Strategic change
- Education and training
- Communication

1.3.4. TQM Principles

There are eight quality management principles on which the quality management system standards of the ISO 9000 series are based. These principles are elaborated below [International Organization for Standardization (2012)]

Leadership

Effective leadership is very important for a successful TQM implementation by an organization. Top management should be committed to continuous quality improvement of their products/services. They need to have clear vision and understanding about the planned strategy with defined set goals. They should act as coach and facilitator to their employees. For this, they require effective communication and humanitarian approach towards their employee to gain their confidence. Some of the key benefits are:

a. People will understand and be motivated towards the organization's goals and objectives

b. Activities are evaluated, aligned and implemented in a unified way

c. Miscommunication between levels of an organization will be minimized.

This principle mandates for

a. Considering the needs of all interested parties including customers, owners, employees, suppliers, financiers, local communities and society as a whole

b. Establishing a clear vision of the organization's future

c. Setting challenging goals and targets

d. Creating and sustaining shared values, fairness and ethical role models at all levels of the organization

e. Establishing trust and eliminating fear

f. Providing people with the required resources,

training and freedom to act with responsibility and accountability

g. Inspiring, encouraging and recognizing people's contributions.

Customer Satisfaction

The planned strategy and chain of action to be adopted should be focused on the customer. The customer could be internal or external. There should be a mechanism for customer feedback on the products/ services offered by the organization. Also, it is important

a. to discover customer dissatisfaction,
b. to know customer priorities of quality, price, delivery
c. to compare performance with competitors
d. to Identify customer's needs
e. to determine opportunities for improvement

Some of the key benefits are:

a. Increased revenue and market share obtained through flexible and fast responses to market opportunities
b. Increased effectiveness in the use of the organization's resources to enhance customer satisfaction
c. Improved customer loyalty leading to repeat business.

This principle mandates for

a. Researching and understanding customer needs and expectations
b. Ensuring that the objectives of the organization are linked to customer needs and expectations
c. Communicating customer needs and expectations throughout the organization
d. Measuring customer satisfaction and acting on the results

e. Systematically managing customer relationships

f. Ensuring a balanced approach between satisfying the regular customers and other interested parties (such as owners, employees, suppliers, financiers, local communities and society as a whole).

Employee Involvement

TQM calls for the participation of all the personnel coming from top to bottom level of organizational structure. For this, they should be trained on required skills to improve their efficiency and comfort to the changing environment. They must realize their importance in the organizational structure and work as a responsible employee and contribute effectively in the quality improvement. There must be some motivational training programs and provision for additional incentive schemes for the employees.

Some of the key benefits are:

a. Motivated, committed and involved people within the organization

b. Innovation and creativity in furthering the organization's objectives

c. People being accountable for their own performance

d. People eager to participate in and contribute to continual improvement.

This mandates for

a. People understanding the importance of their contribution and role in the organization

b. People identifying constraints to their performance

c. People accepting ownership of problems and their responsibility for solving them

d. People evaluating their performance against their personal goals and objectives

e. People actively seeking opportunities to enhance their competence, knowledge and experience

f. People freely sharing knowledge and experience
g. People openly discussing problems and issues.

Continuous Process Improvement

An organization should work in the direction of continuous quality improvement. For this, they need to continuously work on their process improvement which can be done effectively through reducing number of resources involved, errors occurred, user feedback- to know their satisfaction level and workflow which is conducive for the employees. Some of the key benefits are:

a. Performance advantage through improved organizational capabilities
b. Alignment of improvement activities at all levels to an organization's strategic intent
c. Flexibility to react quickly to opportunities.

This principle mandates for

a. Employing a consistent organization-wide approach to continual improvement of the organization's performance
b. Providing people with training in the methods and tools of continual improvement
c. Making continual improvement of products, processes and systems an objective for every individual in the organization
d. Establishing goals to guide, and measures to track, continual improvement
e. Recognizing and acknowledging improvements.

Supplier Partnership

On an average, 40% of the organizational activities are dependent on external agencies or suppliers in industrial sectors. Thus, an organization also needs to ensure that their supplier's quality is outstanding. They need to work in close association and develop partnering relationship where they equally share the loss or profit based on failure or success of a product or service. Some of the key benefits identified are –

a. Increased ability to create value for both parties
b. Flexibility and speed of joint responses to changing market or customer needs and expectations
c. Optimization of costs and resources.

This principle mandates for

a. Establishing relationships that balance short-term gains with long-term considerations
b. Pooling of expertise and resources with partners
c. Identifying and selecting key suppliers
d. Clear and open communication
e. Sharing information and future plans
f. Establishing joint development and improvement activities
g. Inspiring, encouraging and recognizing improvements and achievements by suppliers.

Process Approach

A desired result is achieved more efficiently when activities and related resources are managed as a process.

Some of the key benefits of Process approach are:

a. Lower costs and shorter cycle times through effective use of resources
b. Improved, consistent and predictable results
c. Focused and prioritized improvement opportunities.

Implementation of this principle will lead to

a. Systematically defining the activities necessary to obtain a desired result
b. Establishing clear responsibility and accountability for managing key activities

c. Analysing and measuring of the capability of key activities

d. Identifying the interfaces of key activities within and between the functions of the organization

e. Focusing on the factors – such as resources, methods, and materials – that will improve key activities of the organization

f. Evaluating risks, consequences and impacts of activities on customers, suppliers and other interested parties.

System approach to management

For an organization, identifying, understanding and managing interrelated processes as a system is important as they contributes to the organization's effectiveness and efficiency in achieving its objectives.

Some of the key benefits that can be derived through system approach to management are:

a. Integration and alignment of the processes that will best achieve the desired results

b. Ability to focus effort on the key processes

c. Providing confidence to interested parties as to the consistency, effectiveness and efficiency of the organization.

Implementation of this principle will lead to

a. Structuring a system to achieve the organization's objectives in the most effective and efficient way

b. Understanding the interdependencies between the processes of the system

c. Structured approaches that harmonize and integrate processes

d. Providing a better understanding of the roles and responsibilities necessary for achieving common objectives and thereby reducing cross-functional barriers

e. Understanding organizational capabilities and establishing resource constraints prior to action

f. Targeting and defining how specific activities within a system should operate

g. Continually improving the system through measurement and evaluation.

Factual approach to decision making

Effective decisions are based on the analysis of data and information. All the activities done by an organization should be quantified and measured for effective management. Some of the key benefits are:

a. Informed decisions

b. An increased ability to demonstrate the effectiveness of past decisions through reference to factual records

c. Increased ability to review, challenge and change opinions and decisions.

This principle mandates for

a. Ensuring that data and information are sufficiently accurate and reliable

b. Making data accessible to those who need it

c. Analysing data and information using valid methods

d. Making decisions and taking action based on factual analysis, balanced with experience and intuition.

Benchmarking, statistical measures such as control charts and an ISO certification are some of the possible performance measures that can be taken into consideration in this regard.

1.3.5. TQM Tools

A. Quality Improvement Teams

According to Thessaloniki (2006), Quality Improvement Teams (QIT) is also known as Process

Improvement Teams or a wide array of other names, are now in-place in many private and public sector organizations. They may be management or self directed. A well managed team process, tied with other quality programs can make an organization more viable while empowering employees to find solutions and opportunities. Management has to believe in the quality team process, listen to proposals and enable feasible solutions to be progressed through pilot stages and into full operation. Open-mindedness is essential. There exist many different types of teams within an organization. Some of them are:

1. Intact work groups : These are responsible for day to day work. Employees are hired based on job requirement. They need to comply with organization's procedures, policies and guidelines. There is Performance Appraisal System for performance evaluation of the employees. They receive paychecks, travel vouchers, sick leave, etc. as rewards/remuneration.

2. Problem-solving : They are responsible to solve specific problem(s); implement solutions: measure/ evaluate outcomes and redefine solutions and disbanded later on. Members from Intact work group are with comprehensive knowledge of the process with a vision and temperament to solve the problem. They generally comprise of 6-8 members. They define problem solving steps using process flowcharts, cause and effect chart, SPC charts, summaries/reports etc. and derive solution to check the problem in the process.

3. Pro-active or implementation teams : They are formed to implement specific process/system. They evaluate the performance and improve upon the loopholes. They work on continuous improvement of the system or process. They comprise of selected members from the Intact work groups and Problem-solving.

4. Small group as used in Japanese companies: Small group activities are developed on Japanese companies vested with the responsibility to improve quality process. Most known groups are:

4(a). Cross-functional Teams

A cross-functional team assembled for a Kaizen (continuous improvement) event is responsible for attaining the results targeted by the team itself. A Kaizen event is a project in which a specific area or manufacturing process has been identified as the target for improvement. The team leader is more concerned with "how" his or her team works rather than "what" the team produces. Solutions are sought as a team, even if a problem has to do with only one member, which reflects the Kaizen process-oriented approach.

4(b). Quality Circle

A group of staff who meet regularly to discuss quality related work problems so that they may examine and generate solutions to these. The circle is empowered to promote and bring the quality improvements through to fruition. Thus, the adoption of quality circles (quality improvement team) has a social focus. There must be commitment from senior management, unit management and supervision, other staff and of course the circle members.

B. Benchmarking

Benchmarking is defined as "the process of identifying and learning from best practices anywhere in the world" (Allan, 1997). The essence of benchmarking is the process of identifying the highest standards of excellence for products, services, or processes, and then making the improvements necessary to reach those standards, commonly called "best practices" [Elmuti, Dean and Kathawala, Yunus (1997)]. Benchmarking was first adopted in the late 1970s by Xerox Corporation to compare its operations with those of its competitors to improve upon its quality standards. Some of the benefits of benchmarking are:

a. It helps in increasing the productivity and improvement on product design

b. Provides an edge over the competitors

c. It provides new perspective on an existing situation, hence, enhances learning and experience

d. It is a tool for performance assessment of an organization

e. It is also a tool for continuous improvement

There are four different types of benchmarking:

Internal benchmarking : It is the benchmarking of similar programs in different sections of an organization.

Competitive benchmarking : It is done externally with the direct competitors (having similar products and services) of the organization. Being the direct competitors, they may not be willing to share and contribute in the process.

Industry or Functional benchmarking : It is similar to competitive benchmarking except for the fact that the benchmarking is done against industry leaders. Not being the direct competitors, they will be more willing to share and contribute in the process.

Process or Generic benchmarking : It attempts to draw best work process or practices that might be uniformly adopted by similar nature organizations. Thus, it involves broad conceptualization of the entire process of work and understanding of all existing procedures and practices.

C. Statistical process control

Montgomery, D.C. (1997) has defined Statistical Process Control (SPC) as"...a powerful collection of problem-solving tools useful in achieving process stability and improving capability through the reduction of variability." Control charts and process capability analysis are the two primary tools of SPC. Other tools such as histograms, flow charts, cause-and-effect diagrams, check sheets, and Pareto diagrams also are useful in quality and process improvement [Leavengood, S. and Reeb, J. (1999)].

Classical tools for quality and process improvement are given below:

Table 2: Statistical Quality Tools

Tool	*Use*
Flowchart	Portrays all the steps in a process. Helps understand the process.
Cause and Effect Diagram	Portrays possible causes of a process problem. Helps determine root cause.
Control Chart	Shows if a process has too much variation.
Histogram	Portrays the frequency of occurrence.
Check Sheet	Tabulates frequency of occurrence.
Pareto Diagram	Visually portrays problems and causes in order of severity or frequency. Helps determine which problem or cause to tackle first.
Scatter Diagram	Helps determine if two variables are related.
Run Chart	Shows variation and trends with time. Provides baseline data, and helps to determine if a process is improving or not.
Stratification	Separation of data into different levels (based on duration, experience, etc.) for analysis.

D. Commitment

In order to make a project successful, it is essential that each member associated with an organisation is committed. Management commitment is clearly a key factor which must be present before initiating an implementation process and employee commitment is necessary as they are actually responsible for the execution of activities during the implementation [Hansson, J., Backlund, Fredrik and Lycke, Liselott (2003)].

E. Training

Training must be a part of the organization's succession planning in order to meet their future goals and objectives. Achieving quality requires constant learning for everyone in an organization, and that learning needs to be part of the organizational culture. Not only should staff members be learning from others in the organization, but they should also be encouraged to take courses, to attend organization-sponsored trainings and workshops, to visit other organizations, etc., to continually learn more about their work, and to get new ideas and perspectives on it [Work Group for Community Health and Development (2014)].

Management must promote the need for continuous training, as it will facilitate the following:

1. Performance enhancement of the employees
2. Employees will be more confident and motivated in their work
3. Reduce staff turnover as the existing number of staff will be able to handle the new project
4. Errors can be reduced as the trained staff can scrutinize the proposed work flow and practices and will be able to suggest modifications
5. In turn, the overall productivity can be improved
6. Improve the organizational competitiveness

1.3.6. Benefits of TQM

The major benefits of TQM in terms of cost savings include:

a. Elimination of non-confirmation and repetitive work
b. Elimination of waste costs and reject products
c. Elimination of repairs and reworks
d. Reduced warranty and customer support costs
e. Process efficiency leading to improved profit per product or service

f. Fiscal discipline through elimination of unnecessary steps and wasteful expenditure

Customer satisfaction oriented benefits

a. Improvement in product quality
b. Improvement in product design
c. Improvement in production flow
d. Improvement in employee morale and quality consciousness
e. Improvement in product service
f. Improvement in market place acceptance

Economic improvement oriented benefits

a. Reduction in operating costs
b. Reduction in operating losses
c. Reduction in field service costs
d. Reduction in liability exposure

For Management

a. Provides an invaluable problem-solving tool for managers and supervisors to use
b. Dispels negative attitudes
c. Management becomes more aware of problems that affect the individual's work environment
d. Employees gain a sense of participation
e. Increases efficiency and productivity
f. Reduces turnover rate, tardiness, costs, errors,and scrap & rework
g. Improves communications within and among all departments
h. Develops management skills that were never taught, or are long forgotten due to lack of
i. application

j. Develops overall company awareness and company unity

k. Rearranges priorities which once seemed locked in place

l. Builds loyalty to the company

m. Reveals training requirements in all departments

n. Lessens the number of defects received from suppliers when they are encouraged to train in quality management

For Employees

a. Provides opportunity for personal growth and development (as a result of team training activities) and the opportunity to develop and present recommendations

b. Increases innovation (through a greater variety of approaches and perspectives) for solving problems, removing fear of failure

c. Employees use their knowledge and skills to generate data-driven recommendations that will lead to well-informed decision making

d. Encourages decision-making at the most appropriate level

e. Increases motivation and acceptance of new ideas

f. Increases job satisfaction (as a result of the opportunity to participate in and have influence over work)

g. Recognizes employees for their knowledge, skills, and contribution toward improvement

h. Develops mutual respect among employees, management and customers

i. Promotes teamwork.

1.5. SIX SIGMA

Six Sigma is an organization-wide approach used

to specify exactly how organization managers set up and achieve objectives. The Six Sigma methodology goes beyond the improvement process and tools because it requires an intelligent use of data, emphasis of statistical analysis and designed experiments. Six Sigma prescribes an improvement process known as DMAIC methodology [Sokoviæ, M., et.al. (2009)]:

- **Define :** improvement of project goals, goals based on customer needs and wants
- **Measure :** current process and establish metrics to monitor the path to achievement of goals
- **Analyze :** current process to understand problems and their causes
- **Improve :** process by identifying and piloting solutions to problems
- **Control :** improved process with standardization and ongoing monitoring.

EXERCISES

1. Give a historical account of the concept "Quality".
2. What is TQM? Why it is required?
3. Explain the concepts:
   a. Product
   b. Customer
4. Discuss various elements of TQM in detail.
5. Enlist eight principles of TQM.
6. Which TQM principle do you consider as crucial in Quality Management in an academic library scenario?
7. Write a short note on various qualitative TQM tools.
8. Explain the importance of Quality Improvement Teams in TQM.
9. What is Benchmarking? Enlist various types of benchmarking.
10. Enlist various statistical quality tools.
11. What are the benefits of TQM?
12. Write a short note on Six Sigma.

13. What do you understand with the term "freedom from deficiencies.
14. Elaborate the concept of "fitness for use" in content of quality in libraries.
15. What do you understand with term "Customer Satisfaction" in content to the libraries.

2

Different Approaches to Total Quality Management

2.1. WALTER A. SHEWHART (1920S -1940S)

Walter A. Shewhart was the first who successfully integrated the disciplines of statistics, engineering, and economics and known as the father of modern quality control. He is most widely known for his "control chart", also called as process-behavior chart, is a simple but highly effective tool that represented an initial step towards what he called "the formulation of a scientific basis for securing economic control."

It was understood by then (during 1920s) that continual process-adjustment in reaction to non-conformance actually leads to increased variation and degraded quality. A control chart was effective to analyze common (assignable) and special (un-assignable) causes of variation. If analysis of the control chart indicates that the process is currently under control (i.e., is stable, with variation only coming from sources common to the process), then no corrections or changes to process control parameters are needed or desired. In addition, data from the process can be used to predict the future performance of the process. If the chart indicates that the monitored process is not in control, analysis of the chart can help determine the sources of variation, as this will result in degraded process performance.

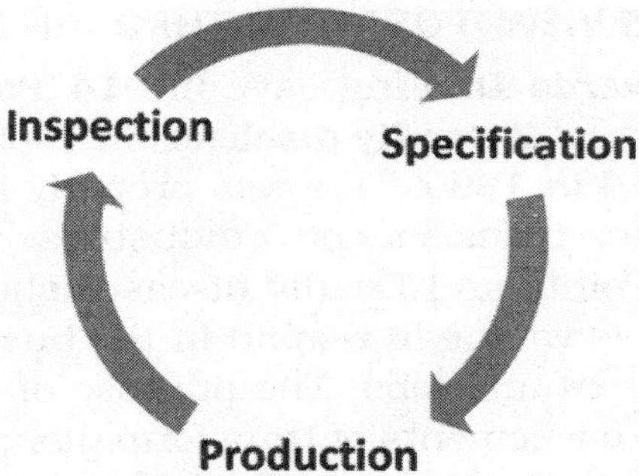

Fig. 1. Shewhart's Cycle

Shewhart's monumental work, *Economic Control of Quality of Manufactured Product*, published in 1931, is regarded as a complete and thorough exposition of the basic principles of quality control. He actually tested on the then existing philosophy that the statistical methodologies can be applied to biological and technical systems. He has also authored *Statistical Method from the Viewpoint of Quality Control* (1939) and served as editor for *Mathematical Statistics Series* for more than two decades. He defined quality in terms of objective and subjective quality. According to him, objective quality is "quality of a thing independent of people" whereas subjective quality is defined in terms of its relation to how people perceive it (or its value to them). Shewhart described manufacture under "control"—under statistical control—as a three-step process of specification, production, and inspection [Figure 1]. According to him, "These three steps must go in a circle instead of in a straight line, as shown . . . It may be helpful to think of the three steps in the mass production process as steps in the scientific method. In this sense, specification, production, and inspection correspond respectively to making a hypothesis, carrying out an experiment, and testing the hypothesis. The three steps constitute a dynamic scientific process of acquiring knowledge."

2.2. DEMING'S VIEW (POST WWII THROUGH 1980S)

W. Edwards Deming gave his **14 Points** for the management and **7 Deadly diseases**, in 1986, which was further revised in 1990. This was properly implemented in Japanese top management & industries. The adoption of these 14 Points and Deadly diseases shows that the management is willing to remain in the business and to protect investors and jobs. The purpose of these points is to explain the elements of transformation, particularly for the western style. The revised **14 Points** are as follows:

1. Create consistency of purpose toward improvement of product and service, with the aim to become competitive and to stay in business, and to provide jobs.

   Revised Version : Create and publish all employees a statement of the aims and purpose of the company or other organization. The management must demonstrate constantly their commitment to this statement.

2. Adopt the new philosophy. We are in a new economic age. Western management must awaken to the challenge, must learn their responsibilities, and take on leadership for change.

   Revised Version : Learn the new philosophy, top management and everybody.

3. Cease dependence on inspection to achieve quality. Eliminate the need for inspection on a mass basis by building quality into the product in the first place.

   Revised Version : Understand the purpose of

inspection, for improvement of processes and reduction of cost.

4. End the practice of awarding business of the basis of price tag. Instead, minimize the total cost. Move towards a single supplier for any one item, on a long-term relationship of loyalty and trust.

   Revised Version : End the practice of awarding business on the basis on price tag alone.

5. Improve constantly and forever the system of production and service, to improve quality and productivity, and thus constantly decrease costs.

   Revised Version : Improve constantly and forever the system of production and service.

6. Institute training on the job.

   Revised Version : Institute training.

7. Institute leadership. The aim of supervision should be to help people and machines and gadgets to do a better job. Supervision of management is in need of overhaul, as well as supervision of production workers.

   Revised Version : Teach and institute leadership.

8. Drive out fear, so that everyone may work effectively for the company.

   Revised Version: Drive out fear, create trust. Create a climate for innovation.

9. Break down barriers between departments. People in research and design, sales, and production must work as a team, to foresee problems of production and in use that may be encountered with the product or service.

   Revised Version: Optimize towards the aims and purposes of the company the efforts of teams, groups, staff areas.

10. Eliminate slogans, exhortations, and targets for the

work force asking for the zero defects and new levels of productivity. Such exhortations only create adversarial relationships, as the bulk of the causes of low quality and low productivity belong to the system and thus lie beyond the power of the work force.

Revised Version: eliminate exhortation for the work force.

11a. Eliminate work standards (quotas) on the factory floor. Substitute leadership.

Revised Version: Eliminate numerical quotas for production. Instead, learn and institute methods for improvement.

11b. Eliminate management by objective. Eliminate management by numbers, numerical goals. Substitute leadership.

Revised Version : Eliminate management by objective. Instead, learn the capabilities of the system, and how to improve them.

12a. Remove barriers that rob the hourly worker of his right to pride of workmanship. The responsibility of supervisors must be change from sheer numbers of quality.

12b. Remove barriers that rob people in management and in engineering of their right to pride of workmanship. This means, inter alia, abolishment of the annual or merit rating and of management by objective.

Revised Version : Remove barriers that rob people of pride of workmanship.

13. Institute a vigorous program of education and self-improvement.

Revised Version : Encourage education and self-improvement for everyone.

14. Put everybody in the company to work to accomplish the transformation.

    Revised Version : Take action to accomplish the transformation.

Enumeration of 7 Deadly Diseases

1. The crippling disease : Lack of consistency of purpose. There is often lack of consistency of purpose in planning and service, which will keep the company in business and in market, and provide jobs.

2. Emphasis on short term profits : It is just opposite to the consistency of purpose, where people don't think on the long lasting aims, it basically comes through, the unfriendly take over or by push of the bankers or the owners for dividends.

3. Evaluation of performance, merit rating, or annual review : Management by Objective, focuses on the objective not on the method for accomplishment of the objective, This may affect the end result if proper attention is not given on the process of improvement. Also, there is tendency among managers to reward people who cooperate more or who seem to have better attitudes, and will insist that they can recognize the people who are most cooperative and have the highest work ethic. Instead, managers should understand that the best way to develop cooperation is by focusing on the nature of work environment, not monetary rewards.

4. Mobility of job – Job Hopping : This occurs when the top management changes organizations every 3-4 years. This paralyzes the continuous improvement efforts.

5. Running the company on visible figures alone (counting the money) : Management by using only visible figures, with little or no consideration of figures that are unknown or unknowable.

6. Excessive medical costs : For the economy as a

whole, health care as a percentage of overall expenditures has steadily risen for decades, which gradually pushes numerous businesses into a state of crisis. Potentially the only remedy for this disease would be a political system attempting to reform health care.

7. Excessive cost of liability : This aspect is swelled up by lawyers that work on contingency fees and spend much of their time to find people to sue, crippling the development programs. The remedy has to come from the government.

PDCA or Stewhart's Cycle

Different organizations have adopted different methodologies, tools and techniques for continuous improvement in their performance. Dr. J. Edward Deming modified Shewhart cycle in 1951 into four step process:

Step 1 – Design

Step 2 – Produce

Step 3 – Sell and

Step 4 – Redesign through marketing research.

These four steps were re-casted by Japanese authorities as PDCA Cycle, which they referred to as Deming Cycle. PDCA is an acronym for Plan, Do, Check and Act. Deming Cycle provides conceptual as well as practical framework while carrying out continuous improvement (Kaizen: Japanese word for "continuous improvement") activities by the employees.

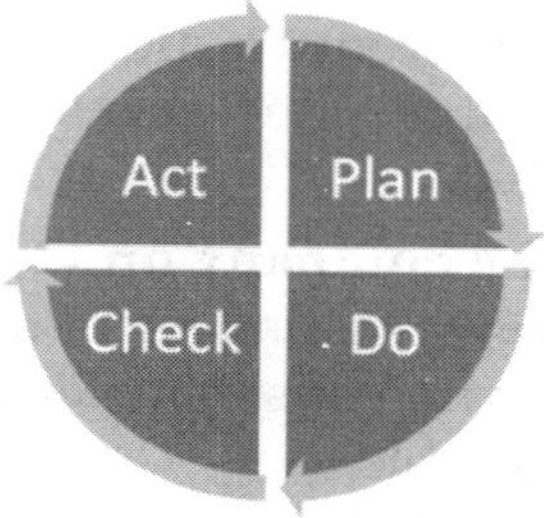

Fig. 2. The PDCA or Deming's Cycle

1. **PLAN** stage involves analyzing the current situation, gathering data, and developing ways to make improvements.
2. The **DO** stage involves testing alternatives experimentally in a laboratory establishing a pilot process, or trying it out with small number of customers.
3. The **CHECK** stage requires determining whether the trial or process is working as intended, whether any revisions are needed, or whether is should be scrapped.
4. The **ACT** stage focuses on implementing the process within the organization or with its customers and suppliers.

Once all this stages are completed to the fullest satisfaction, the improvement is standardized. The standardized work or product is the result of improvement initiative but it is not stopped here. With the changing circumstances or new techniques this standardized work, process, product or service is again subjected to further improvement thus repeating the Deming Cycle again and again [Nameer (2009)]. Deming again modified the Shewhart cycle in 1993 and called it the Shewhart cycle for learning and improvement- the PDSA cycle. He described it as a flow diagram for learning, and for improvement of a product or of a process.

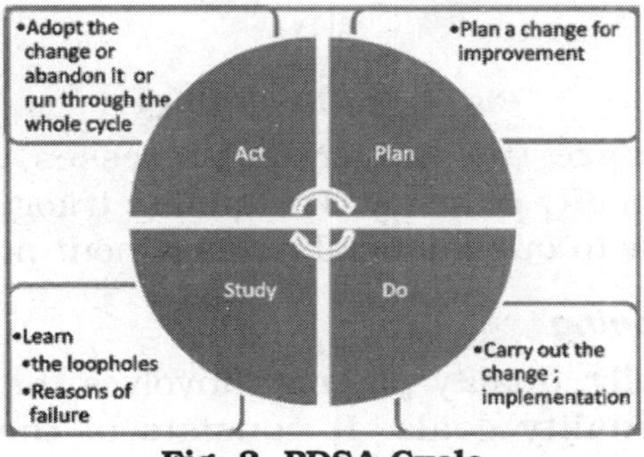

Fig. 3. PDSA Cycle

2.3. J.M. JURAN'S VIEW (CONSULTANT POST WWII THROUGH 1980S)

Juran is considered as one of the great philosophers having a strong impact on the evolution of the concept quality. He echoed the Deming's philosophy; nevertheless, with some differences. While Deming emphasized the need for organizational transformation, Juran believed that implementation of quality initiatives does not need dramatic changes [Evans, James R. and Lindsay, William M. (2010)].

J. M. Juran in his famous article **'The Quality Trilogy'** in Quality Progress, August 1986 conceived the concept of Quality Trilogy. According to him the managing of quality depends on the three basic processes:

- Quality planning
- Quality control
- Quality improvement

Fig. 4. Quality Trilogy

These are the universal processes, which are applicable in any industry. The quality trilogy process is quite similar to our financial management process.

Quality Planning

Basically, quality planning involves the process to meet the quality goals. It consists of the following processes:

- Identify the customers, both external and internal
- Determine customers needs
- Develop product features that responds to customers' needs
- Establish quality goals that meet the needs of customer and supplier alike, and do so at minimum combined cost.
- Develop a process that can produce the needed product features
- Prove process capability- prove that the process can meet the quality goals under operating conditions.

The usual starting point for this is to set up a Quality Planning Council, which will be working parallel to the company's Budgeting committee. This committee will formulate the corporate quality policies, quality goals and breaking these goals in the major divisions and provision of infrastructure for the quality plan.

Quality Control

It consists of the process of meeting the quality goals, under the operating conditions. Quality control involves the following process:

- Choose control subjects- what to control
- Choose units of measurement
- Establish measurement
- Establish standards of performance
- Measure actual performance
- Interpret the difference (actual verses standard)
- Take action on the difference

The quality planning council has to review the performance of the company time to time against their set plans and goals. The measurement of the performance includes measurement of marketing, productivity etc. But it is difficult to measure these properties, which are abstract. For those properties **Juran** suggested to measure the number of non-conformities.

Quality improvement

It includes the process for the unprecedented levels of performance. It includes the following processes:

- Prove the need of improvement
- Identify the specific projects for improvement
- Organize to guide the projects
- Organize for diagnosis- for discovery of causes
- Diagnosis to find the causes
- Provide remedies
- Prove that the remedies are effective under operating conditions
- Provide for control to hold the gains

For this the company has to conduct regular training programs. The employees should be given the extensive training on the quality trilogy. They should be informed about the use of statistical process to measure their performance and use of quality circles. Employee participation through quality circles was strongly recommended by Juran. He is widely credited for adding the human dimension to quality management and emphasized on education and training of managers. As per Juran, problems in human relations and resistance to change were the root cause of quality issues. [Juran, J. M. (1967)]

2.4. ISHIKAWA'S VIEW (POST WWII - 1980s)

Ishikawa was very much influenced with **Deming's** and **Juran's** view. However, he made it a bit different from the normal view of both.

Emphasis on Quality Assurance

When **Juran** delivered the lecture to the Japanese about the quality control, another concept called "quality assurance" came up in to the picture. Earlier the concept of quality assurance was restricted only to the inspection of the product or services offered. That means none of the defective product should be shipped to their respective customers. However, the idea got broader and the emphasis shifted on **Zero Defects**. For this, it is good to start controlling the factors from very beginning of the product design, production, installation, marketing, purchasing and transporting. So, quality assurance means in an organization, all its divisions and employees must participate in the quality control. The quality control also involves the participation of the subsidiaries of the organization. And, finally the quality assurance should become the organization-wide. He also emphasized on the birth of the Quality Circles. This is quite important because holding seminars, conferences, etc. can be effective in the education of the engineers and staff members. The QC circles are the best method to educate the employees.

Deming has given the four stages of the quality control i.e. the **PDCA cycle**, which represents the plan, do, check and action. Ishikawa elaborated this PDCA cycle by deming as follows :

Planning

1. Determine goals and targets.
2. Determine methods of reaching goals.

Do

3. Engage in education and training.
4. Implement work.

Check

5. Check the effects of implementation.

Action

6. Take appropriate action.

He also emphasized on the use of statistical techniques; particularly he gave more emphasis on Cause and Effect diagram. Ishikawa advocated the use of seven quality tools (discussed under Statistical Process Control of the *section 1.3.5*) developed independently of each other, in the Quality circles of Japan during their quality revolution.

2.5. CROSBY'S VIEW (1980s)

Philip B. Crosby's name is best known in relation to the concepts of **Do It Right First time** and **Zero Defects**. He considers traditional quality control, acceptable quality limits and waivers of sub-standard products/services to represent failure rather than assurance of success. Crosby, therefore, defines quality as conformance to the requirements, which the company itself has established for its products, based directly on its customers' needs. He believed that since most companies have organizations and systems that allow deviation from what is really required, manufacturing companies spend around 20% of their revenues doing things wrong and doing them over again. According to Crosby, this can be 35% of operating expenses for service companies.

He does not believe that workers should take prime responsibility for poor quality; the reality, he says, is that you have to get management straight. In the Crosby scheme of things, management sets the tone on quality and workers follow their example; whilst employees are involved in operational difficulties and draw them to management's attention, the initiative comes from the top (management). **Zero defects** means that the company's objective is 'doing things right first time'. This will not prevent people from making mistakes, but will encourage everyone to improve continuously.

In the Crosby approach, the Quality Improvement message is spread by creating a core of quality specialists within the company. There is strong emphasis on the top-down approach, since he believes that senior management is entirely responsible for quality.

The ultimate goal is to train all the staff and give them the tools for quality improvement, to apply the basic precept of Prevention Management in every area. This is aided by viewing all work as a process or series of actions conducted to produce a desired result. A process model can be used to ensure that clear requirements have been defined and understood by both the supplier and the customer. He also views quality improvement as an ongoing process since the work 'programme' implies a temporary situation. Crosby's Quality Improvement Process is based upon the **Four Absolutes of Quality Management**:

1. Quality is defined as conformance to requirements, not as 'goodness' or 'elegance'.
2. The system for causing quality is prevention, not appraisal.
3. The performance standard must be Zero Defects, not "that's close enough".
4. The measurement of quality is the Price of Nonconformance, not indices.

Crosby's 14 points for the Quality Improvement

He has given *14 points for the quality improvement.* These points are:

1. Management commitment
2. Quality improvement team
3. Quality measurement
4. Cost of evaluation
5. Quality awareness
6. Corrective action
7. Establish an ad hoc committee for the Zero Defect

8. Supervisor training
9. Zero Defect Day
10. Goal setting
11. Error cause removal
12. Recognition
13. Quality council
14. Do it over again

2.6. TAGUCHI'S VIEW (1960S - 1980s)

Dr. Genichi Taguchi gave the concept of **Robust Design**. Actually the aim of it was to develop the product which has minimum variation. Robust design uses the mathematical methods for the design of experiments. According to him quality can be measured in terms of the loss done by the product to the society, due to functional variation. The basic aim of the **Robust Design** is to minimize the operating cost, manufacturing cost and R&D cost. The fundamental of the **Robust Design** is to minimize the effect of the causes without removing the causes. This is known as parameter design. However, good environment and tools and techniques for operation and inspection are vital to support it. Two important jobs we do in **Robust Design**:

- Measure the quality during design/ development
- Efficient experimentation to find the optimum design parameters.

2.7. COMPARISON OF DIFFERENT VIEWS

As we understand with different views of one thing is common in all of them i.e., customer's-satisfaction. Starting with Steward's 3 step ****** quality control, he gave a two directional approach towards quality (subjective and objective) judging the quality independent of customer and considering the user perception on another hand. The basic approach of **Deming, Juran, Ishikawa** and **Crosby** is quite similar. **Deming's** *14 points* can also be seen in the **Juran's** approach of quality by quality planning, quality control and quality improvement. **Deming** particularly talks about the removal of fear from the employees and use of statistics for the measurement. **Juran** has also given emphasis on the use of statistics and the measurement of the quality by using the indicators, but primarily he uses the cost as the indicator of quality. **Crosby** also has similar approach. Basically, **Crosby**, **Deming** and **Juran** all talked much on the role of the management in quality achievement. In the beginning, **Juran** used to talk about the quality in the terms of **"fitness for use"** but later on he shifted his emphasis on 'Customer satisfaction'. Similar approach is also supported by **Taguchi** in his **Robust Design** concept. But he uses quite different method for the quality improvement; with the use of mathematical approach for design of experiment. Particularly *Taguchi's method* needs more precision in the measurement of the parameters, which are responsible for the variation in the product and services. His method is highly dependent on the engineering techniques. **Crosby** measures the quality in the terms of appeared *nonconformance*. He particularly believes in doing the things right in very first approach of the work. One thing, which differentiates him from the others, is his belief that quality can come by prevention. **Ishikawa** has common views from both **Deming** and **Juran**. Ishikawa's thought are just the modifications of both of them, adapted to the Japanese environment. In fact, his views are the actual reflections of the Japan's Quality management strategy.

The principle strength of **Crosby's** program is the commitment of the management to the **Zero Defect**. In his program the management must implement the *fourteen points* given by him. Thus his approach is basically from top to bottom. While, **Deming** with the commitment of the management emphasizes on use of statistical techniques, and thus his way of approach to the quality is bottom to top. Mostly, **Juran's** approach is a sort of mixture of both the approaches. **Taguchi** has entirely different approach for quality, though it is also bottom to top approach, by defining the various parameters, which are affecting the process and see the effect of change in the value of the parameters on the ultimate result.

EXERCISES

1. Define quality as per Crosby?
2. Compare different views of quality gurus.
3. Explain "Quality Trilogy" in context to libraries.
4. Enumerate "7 deadly diseases" in context to quality.
5. Discuss contribution of W.A.Shewhart in "Quality Management".
6. Explain PDCA Cycle or Shewhart Cycle.
7. Write a note on J. M. Juran and his views on quality.
8. Explain Quality Assurance.
9. Enlist Crosby's 14 points of Quality Improvement.
10. Write short note on:
    a. Robust Design
    b. Zero Defects
    c. PDSA Cycle
11. Discuss W.E. Deming's 14 points of management.

3
TQM in Libraries

Globalization has strongly influenced the work culture of different organizations, whether private or public. They all are enforced to adopt every measure that ensures their wider acceptance and maintain competitive edge over their competitors. Indeed, educational institutions, which have been considered as public goods and not-for-profit organizations, have taken up the position of a commercial service. Scholars interested to pursue their studies look for quality in the different services offered by the academic institutions. Libraries largely support learning, teaching and research process; hence, they are one of the most essential components to evaluate any academic institution. In India, the National Assessment and Accreditation Council (NAAC), the government agency to accredit higher education institutions, put a special emphasis on the evaluation of libraries and monitors their collection, services and their outreaching capacity. In the recent past, libraries have made significant developments to improve their user services. They are adopting quality models and standards with an intention to mandate their presence in the ever changing global environment. As far as approach for implementation of TQM is concerned, Düren, Petra (2012) suggests that it is not always necessary to introduce a Quality Management System completely and get certified. A first step might be the implementation of a complaint management system or to analyze and improve separated operational key processes.

3.1. IMPLEMENTATION OF TQM BY LIBRARIES

Quality management has been an integral component of libraries ever since they existed. Performance indicators; performance evaluation; evaluation of reference sources using check-list of criteria; Evaluation of Information Retrieval systems using Precision and Recall rations; Cost-Benefit and costeffectiveness studies; user surveys electing opinions on library services - all these studies make part and parcel of Quality Studies using different mechanisms of assessment and methodologies [Saroja, G and Sujatha, G.]. Mola, Núria Balagué (2007) had conducted an extensive study on the institutions that have received ISO certification of their quality management systems (ISO standard 9001:2000) and examined the reasons for seeking certification and the advantages and difficulties they have encountered in applying this ISO standard. Table 3 depicts the geographic distribution of libraries that have obtained ISO certification.

Table 3. Comparison between the estimated universe and the answers received

	ASIA				EUROPE		
Country	Estimate	Answers	%	Country	Estimate	Answers	%
South Korea	2	1	50,0	Germany	1	0	0,0
Philippines	5	1	20,0	Belgium	1	1	100,0
Georgia	1	0	0,0	Bulgaria	2	2	100,0
India	3	1	33,3	Slovakia	1	1	100,0
Indonesia	1	1	100,0	Spain	9	7	77,8
Israel	1	1	100,0	Finland	1	1	100,0
Macao	2	0	0,0	Italy	5	4	80,0
Malaysia	13	6	46,1	Poland	4	2	50,0

Pakistan	3	1	33,3	Portugal	1	1	100,0
Singapore	3	1	33,3	U.K.	1	0	0,0
Thailand	9	0	0,0	Russia	3	2	66,7
China	1	0	0,0	Turkey	3	2	66,7
Total	44	13	29,5	Total	32	23	71,9

	AMERICA				*AUSTRALIA*		
Country	*Estimate*	*Answers*	*%*	*Country*	*Estimate*	*Answers*	*%*
Argentina	1	1	100,0	Australia	4	3	75,0
Brazil	3	3	100,0	Total	4	3	75,0
Colombia	2	1	50,0				
El Salvador	2	2	100,0				
Honduras	1	1	100,0				
Mexico	28	18	64,3				
Peru	2	1	50,0				
Uruguay	1	0	0,0				
Venezuela	1	1	100,0				
Total	41	28	68,3	Total	121	67	55,4

He also identified various reasons for implementing ISO 9001 by these libraries which are listed on the basis their degree of importance:

1. Goal of improving the quality of library services
2. Strategy of the university in quality issues
3. Need to improve the work systems of the Library
4. Need to improve the organization of the Library
5. Prestige of ISO 9001
6. Users' requirements and expectations
7. Requirements of a government body (e.g. Ministry of Education)
8. Implementation of ISO 9001 in other libraries

Efforts toward the adoption of TQM to improve the library services have already been taken by several libraries. ISO standard has emerged as one of the major management tools for improvement that libraries around the world have adopted in recent years. In United States, Harvard College Library created a task force which rewrote the library's vision statement, and considered changes that would have to be made in order to develop a new organization culture. With the help of consultants, Harvard learned about TQM, and found that its principles of service excellence, teamwork, ongoing training and skill building, process/systems focus, continuous improvement, and cooperation across boundaries could help them make the changes they needed. Also, the Oregon State University Libraries tested TQM. Two small teams, the Shelving Team from the stack maintenance unit, and the Documents Team from the government publications unit worked with outside facilitators. Each team surveyed users and staff and found that some issues, perceived as critical by staff, were not perceived as critical by customers and therefore needed rethinking in terms of TQM. The Shelving Team, which wanted to address the problem of long-lasting shelving backlogs, found that the shelvers, who worked alone on the floors, felt isolated and unmotivated to make progress. Using this information, the team devised a plan for shelvers to work in small groups and have an assigned floor. The result was an increased "espirit de corps," tidier shelves, and less backlog [Butcher, K. S. (1993)]. Düren, Petra (2012) has reported some of the quality management projects in Germany and explains the first steps of Quality Management in two academic libraries namely, Medical Library of the University Medical Center Hamburg-Eppendorf and University Library of the Helmut-Schmidt-University.

As far as Indian scenario is concerned, the Central Library at IIT Madras participated in the ISO-9001 certification process along with other units of the Institute. During this process a detailed systems and procedures manual was prepared and submitted to the Management of the Institute. Various quality auditing, internal as well as external, were conducted and non conformity reports were responded immediately. The final certification team also visited and scrutinized the entire written systems and procedures of the Central Library with other units of the Institute and certified the library with ISO-9001 standard. In 2008, Asiatic Society of India got ISO 9001 certification under the American National Accreditation Board. Allama Iqbal Library, Kashmir University is the first University Library in India to get ISO 9001:2008 certification for its library services.

It is evident from the above study that quality assurance studies were mostly restricted to special libraries and academic libraries. Also, quality assurance studies based on ISO 9001 and other accreditation schemes were conducted more extensively by the libraries in United States, Europe, Asia and Australia but none of the libraries from African continent has been reported to obtained ISO certification. In Asia, Malaysian libraries are moving ahead and many libraries have reported to acquired ISO certification. As far as Indian scenario is concerned, the effort is keeping very low pace. An organized effort is required to make people know about the importance of standardization and raise awareness about quality assurance for libraries.

3.2. CHARACTERISTICS OF A QUALITY LIBRARY SERVICE

The various characteristics enlisted below are intertwined with each other and lack of one or many may lead to loss of actual or potential user.

a. Credibility and Reliability : This factor is one the most influential factor for any service based sector. A service organization like library need to establish an environment which creates a complete dependability of their library users on the library for their information needs and demands.

b. Efficiency : Efficiency of a library service can be judged through the response time taken by a library staff to a user query. As more is the response time to a query, lesser will be the possibility for the library to retain their users. For this, libraries need to re-evaluate their existing collection strength against the objective of their institution as well as their services to bring down their response time. Use of ICT technologies should be encouraged in this regard. Purchase of online journals, e-books should be encouraged for simultaneous access of a resource to many users. Implementation of digital libraries and automation of library house-keeping operation are some of the options available for the libraries to improve their services.

c. Security : Implementation of CCTV camera and Electro Magnetic gate are some of the measures to track the inflow and outflow of library books and also mishandling of library books by users to strengthen the security of library resources.

d. Effectiveness : Evaluation of library collection and services should be done periodically to understand their effectiveness in catering their user's needs. It is important to improvise methods which can lead to effective library services.

e. Congeniality : A library user should feel comfortable to approach to a library staff for their information needs. The environment within the library should be conducive and library staff should have friendly behavior with their user.

f. Privacy : Privacy is one of the major factors for quality services by libraries. A user may not like to share his borrowing details with other users of the library. Hence, libraries need to clearly define their privacy policies for their library users so that the user may know what could be the extent of breach of his/her privacy by the libraries. This is important to gain the confidence of their library users.

Libraries need to ensure that the factors listed above are taken into consideration while framing library policies and procedures.

3.3. ISSUES RELATED TO IMPLEMENTATION OF TQM IN LIBRARIES

Jurow, S. & Barnard, S. B. (1993) identified four barriers to the adoption of TQM libraries

1. Vocabulary : Objections to terms such as "total", "quality", and "management" which indicate that high standards are not already being met by the organization.

2. Commitment : TQM takes several years to implement and requires a long-term commitment by library managers

3. Process : Our culture tends to be impatient and we try to solve problems quickly, contrary to TQM's careful process analysis; and

4. Professionalization : Professional staff can be resistant to turning over their practices and services to what they perceive as the "uninformed whims of the customer".

Miller, R.G. and Stearns, B. (1994) listed the following barriers to the implementation of TQM in libraries:

1. The view that this is just another management fad of the day;
2. Management's fear of the loss control;
3. Employee reluctance to recommend changes because of fear of management;
4. The business and industrial background of TQM might not lend itself to the non-profit sector, including libraries;
5. TQM requires a long-term investment of time over several years as processes are analyzed and
6. An organization's culture is changed – this can cause

resistance; and other difficulties in these days of increasing financial and other pressures

Some scholars have identified rigid organizational structure [Shin, D., Kalinowski, J.G. and El-Enein, G.A. (1998); Wilkinson, A., Redman, T. and Shape, E. (1995)] which has bureaucratic approach and inflexible work culture may cause failure of implementation of TQM. Cultural barrier is also identified as one of the major barriers for TQM implementation [Sohal, A.S., Samson, D. and Ramsay, L. (1998)]; [Tata, J., Prasad, S. and Thorn, R. (1999)]. Research on the culture barrier argues that management values differ significantly across national cultures, that management is culture-specific and that managerial practices, such as TQM, must be tailored to fit the local culture [Bartlett, C.A. and Ghoshal, S. (1992); Trompenaars, F. (1994)]. It is difficult to make a change in organizational structures as TQM requires institutions to restructure. Resistance to change and people's attitudes are primary hindrances to implementing TQM in libraries. The other barriers are the problems of finding the money and time for training while maintaining current services in the library [Moghaddam, Golnessa Galyani and Moballeghi]. Some of the identified barriers to TQM in an organization are [Faisal Talib, Zillur Rahman, M.N. Qureshi, (2011)]:

a. Lack of top management commitment: Management commitment play a crucial role in the implementation of TQM. Lack of top management commitment may stem from various reasons like lack of experience and training, resistance to change, and hesitation in initiating improvement programs. A proper leadership and commitment is essential for the successful implementation of TQM in service sectors like libraries as well as for manufacturing industries.

b. High turnover at management level and Absenteeism : Failure of employees and managers to adopt to new rules and organizational hierarchies; change in organizational work culture; lack of performance appraisal systems such as provision of rewards and training; selection of ineffective employees are some of the reasons that may incur high turnover for the organization and stemming of absenteeism tendency.

c. Attitude of employee towards quality : It is important for an organization to make their employees understand the importance of quality and its effectiveness in improving the productivity/services of the organization. Here, the committed leadership efforts can motivate their employees towards quality.

d. Lack of proper training and education : A successful TQM environment requires a committed, well trained, and educated work force that participates fully in quality improvement activities. Insufficient training on quality as well as training in problem identification and problem solving techniques leads to failure in TQM implementation program.

e. Lack of coordination between departments : TQM demands for a coordinated approach rather than a competitive environment. Thus, various departments of an organization need to work in coordination and maintain health relation among their employees for successful implementation of TQM.

f. Human resource barrier : It is essential to have sufficient human resources as an understaffed and overworked department may not be able to implement TQM successfully. Some other factors for TQM failure are non participation of employees, low knowledge and experience about TQM, lack of culture and geographic homogeneity, lack of non monetary motivation mechanisms, the tedious aspect of writing procedures, and low wages and salaries.

g. No benchmarking : Benchmarking is important for continuous quality improvement. It is a continuous systematic mechanism by an organization where they compare their business practice with those of their competitors, so as to improve their productivity.

h. Poor planning : Low priority to planning by top management may lead to ineffective quality improvement. Careful and detailed planning is important prior to implementation of any quality improvement program where each stage of implementation is identified.

i. Employees' resistance to change : Employees may perceive TQM implementation as a controlling mechanism where there is more work against fewer rewards. The factors influencing the employees behavior could be age (aged people are likely to be afraid and more resistant to change), illiteracy, lack of proper communication, fear (of loss of autonomy or academic freedom in a higher education system).

j. Inadequate use of empowerment and teamwork : There should be sufficient emphasis on teamwork and problem solving groups while implementing TQM. Most of the time these groups are seldom used to their fullest extent and the individual members are often contended. Insufficient teamwork facilitators and absence of team building techniques in the organization may also cause failure of TQM implementation.

k. Lack of continuous improvement culture : An organization should emphasize on continuous improvement culture with a goal of zero defect [Deming, W.E. (1986); Schneider, B., Brief, A.P. and Guzzo, R.A. (1996)]. Al Zamany, Y., Hoddell, E.J. and Savage, B.M. (2002) reported that lack of continuous improvement culture in the organization may be due to the following reasons:

a. unhealthy habits of the managers and executives;

b. weak sense of responsibility of the managers;

c. absence of assessment activities in the organizations;

d. appointment of unqualified managers; and

e. lack of effective action to force improvement

1. Lack of communication : Lack of communication among the team members, in between two departments of an organization, between top management and the employees may result to an environment of distrust and conflict which ultimately may lead to loss in productivity, unsatisfied customer and eventually a total failure of TQM efforts.

3.4. ADVANTAGES OF TQM IN LIBRARIES

User's satisfaction and continuous improvement of the services with available resources are two primary concerns for a library. Some of the benefits of TQM for libraries are [Halkar, G. and K. Govidrajulu (2014)]:

a. Incremental changes lead to continuous improvement unlike quick solutions that may yield only partial results

b. Provides a method of improving services to users in a given period with available resources

c. It helps to break down barriers between library departments and improves communication within the organization

d. More focus on training of staff to harness their skills

e. Inculcating the feeling of "ownership" among employees as TQM mandates for staff participation in decision making

f. Forces library managers to develop leadership quality

g. Removes ambiguity in the work flow as well as in job responsibility

Libraries, being service based organization, have always been committed to provide a high quality services to its users. However, they need to continuously struggle for the resources to meet the changing demands of their users and prove their relevance to the organization. They cannot afford failures in their projects. Thus, TQM is indispensable as far as the libraries are concerned. Through TQM, a library can identify their key processes as well as the areas where improvements are required. It also offers various quantitative and qualitative improvement tools and techniques to check the unassigned variations. Thus, it helps to improve the level of performance through error free processes. It also ensures spontaneous augmentation in the degree of involvement of all the functionaries involved in the process of quality improvement.

EXERCISES

1. Write a note on TQM implementation in Libraries.
2. Discuss various issues related to TQM in libraries.
3. How TQM can help improve the services of the library.
4. What are the advantages of TQM in Libraries?
5. Write a note on the characteristics of quality library service. Can you suggest some more activities to be adopted by the libraries to enhance the quality of their library services?

4

Introduction to ISO-9000

4.1. NEED FOR QUALITY SYSTEM

The phenomenon of globalization has created an environment of competitiveness among various organizations and also raised the expectations of the customers/end users. Earlier, the quality of a product was evaluated on the basis of *percentage of defects*. Now we are talking the defects in *parts per million* or even in *parts per billion*. Thus, the acceptability level for defects has narrowed down towards the zero defects. In such atmosphere, Quality Assurance System Standardization seems to be a must tool.

Standardization is part of life. We seek standard to simplify one job and cross platform operability. In market, potatoes are sold in Kilograms. Kilogram is a standard to measure weight. This is standardization. Different company refills can fit into each other's mosquito repellent machine. 40 watt bulb will consume same amount of power irrespective of their manufacturing company. Different temperature and pressure give different results with the same compounds in Chemical reactions. This is Product Standardization.

Buying the ISI marked bulb. An ISI mark confirms

the efficiency and quality of a product, thus conformance, of making one Kg bulb. It requires heavy inspection and testing. This is Product Standardization and so Product Certification. So, the conformance of product needs Inspection and Testing. Product Certification leads post-production inspection and testing, while Quality Assurance System Standardization believes in prevention quality management.

Services or flexible products are difficult to get the product certification. So, Quality System Certification is necessary. Having a Quality Assurance System Certification saves lot of time and money for buyer and purchaser. Buyer need not to go for inspecting purchaser, once again if the purchaser already had gone for some sort of Quality Assurance System Certification. A well recognized Quality Assurance System can really boost up the world of business.

So, it is obvious to move towards the Quality Assurance System Certification, as it reduces cost of product with increase in the product quality. But it doesn't make Product Certification obsolete. It has its own importance in the products related to safety and public health. But it is important to have Quality Assurance System Certification as we see the dual benefit of it in quality improvement and cost effectiveness.

4.2. ISO AND ITS CONTRIBUTION TO STANDARDIZATION

The conference that established the International Organization of Standardization was held from 14-26 Oct. 1946. ISO was born unifying two organizations ISA (International Federation of Internationalization Association), existed from 1926, administered from Switzerland and UNSCC (United Nation Standard Coordinating Committee), existed from 1944 and administered from London. The Headquarter of the new organization was established at Geneva.

From 1947 onwards ISO has seen many changes

in the world of the standardization. In fifties the motto of the ISO was provisions of recommendations. These recommendations confined to the several industrial sectors, which were already carried out by the organizations like ISA, UNSCC and IES (International Electro-technical Commission), founded in 1906. By this time there were 60 technical committees founded. 1960's, was the time for the depression for ISO. General Assembly meeting had raised questions on the future of ISO. A committee was formed to visualize the role of ISO in future, named as NEDCO. Committee submitted its report in 1966, addressing the need of ISO to form the standards rather recommendations. Result of this change in the thinking brought out several standards like ISBN and standards related to Nuclear Energy.

In 1971 it was decided to have standards for environmental issues. Later two separate Technical Committees formed in the subsequent years for Air Quality and Water Quality. Later on in 1980 there was another committee formed for Solar Energy. Finally, ISO established the ISO Standards for Environmental Management ISO 14000.

From many years ISO was holding debates on Inspection and Testing in its seminars. It was in 1978, a Technical Committee established to bring out the great series of standards named as ISO 9000. The committee named TC/176 is responsible for the development of standards on Quality Management and Quality Assurance, in 1987.

The root of the development of the ISO 9000 started from the MIL-Q-9858 in 1959, imposed by the U.S. Department of Defence on the contractors. Its only revision has been done in 1963, named it as MIL-Q-9858A.

In 1968, North Atlantic Treaty Organization adopted as basis for its series of standards, named as AQAPs

(Allied Quality Assurance Publications) 1, 4, and 9. AQAP-1 was the quality system specification and basically adopted MIL-Q-9858A, and AQAP-4 and AQAP-9 were inspection system specification. Being the member of the NATO Britain did not accepted the AQAPs . The Ministry of Defence in U.K. established a new series of standards named DEF/STAN 05-8, in1970. Later on DEF/STAN has been changed like the current ISO 9000 standards and it is named as DEF/STAN 05-21, 05-22, 05-23 and 05-24, corresponding to ISO 9001, 9002, 9003 and 9004.

In 1987, the TC 176 of ISO developed a series of standards keeping BS 5750 as the basis for it. In the same year ISO 9000 and BS 5750 got harmonized and became equivalent documents. The EC adopted the harmonized standard and was designated European Norm En 29000. In America ASQC (American Society of Quality Control ANSI (American National Standards Institute) established and published the Q-90 series, which is identical to ISO 9000.

4.3. ISO-9000 FAMILY

The ISO 9000 family of standards represent an international consensus on good management practices with the aim of ensuring that the organization can time and again deliver the product or services that meet the client's quality requirements. The family of ISO 9000 standards is made up of four core standards:

a) ISO 9000 – Fundamentals and Vocabulary

b) ISO 9001 – Quality Management Systems – Requirements

c) ISO 9004 – Quality Management Systems – Guidelines for performance improvements

The ISO 9000 family of standards is the exact same standard across the globe even though they are called by different names. Each member country has their own entity authorized by ISO to manage the standards, but they are all the same exact ISO 9000 quality documents and set of requirements. BIS is the National Standards Body of India and is a founder member of ISO. BIS represents India, in ISO. The Technical Committee (TC) number 176 (ISO/TC 176), and its Sub-committees of ISO are responsible for the development of ISO 9000 standards. Quality and industry experts from India including BIS officers nominated by BIS participate in the meetings of the Technical Committee ISO/TC 176 and its Sub-committees. ISO 9001 'Quality Management Systems – Specifications with Guidance for use' is a standard adopted by BIS as IS/ISO 9001. IS/ISO 9001 is the exact replica of ISO 9001. It is a requirements standard. It contains a set of requirements to define the operation of the Quality Management System. Since the requirements are expressed in a general form, it has the flexibility to be applied to any organization.

4.3.1. ISO 9000:2000

ISO 9000:2000 specifies requirements for a quality management system that can be used by an organization to address customer satisfaction, by meeting customer and applicable regulatory requirements. It can also be used by internal and external parties, including certification bodies, to assess the organization's ability to meet customer and regulatory requirements.

The adoption of a quality management system needs to be a strategic decision of the organization. The decision and implementation of an organization's quality management system is influenced by varying needs, particular objectives, the products provided, the processes employed and the size and structure of the organization. It is not the purpose of this International Standard to imply uniformity in the structure of quality management system or uniformity of documentation.

It is emphasized that the quality management requirements specified in this International Standard are complementary to the technical requirements for products.

4.3.2 Changes in ISO 9000:1994 and ISO 9000:2000

Several of the key standards within the current ISO 9000 family of Quality Management and Quality Assurance standards are being revised to form the core of the 2000 ISO 9000 family of standards. These revisions includes :

- The merging of ISO 9001:1994, ISO 9002:1994 and ISO 9003:1994 into a single ISO 9001:2000 standard.
- The merging of ISO 8402 and part of the content of ISO 9000-1 into a new ISO 9000:2000 standard.
- The revision of ISO 9004-1 into a new ISO 9004:2000 standard.

4.3.3. ISO 9000:2000

4.3.3.1. Process approach

This International Standard encourages the adoption of a process approach to quality management.

Any activity that receives input and converts then to outputs can be considered as a process. For organizations to function effectively, they have to identify and manage numerous linked processes. Often the output from one process will be the input for the next process. The systematic identification and management of the processes employed within an organization and the interactions between such processes may be referred to as the 'process approach'.

Figure 5 is a conceptual illustration of one model of the process approach, which shows customers play a significant role in defining requirements as inputs. Monitoring of customers satisfaction is necessary to evaluate and validate whether customer requirements have been met. This model does not reflect processes at a detailed level, but covers all the requirements of this International Standard.

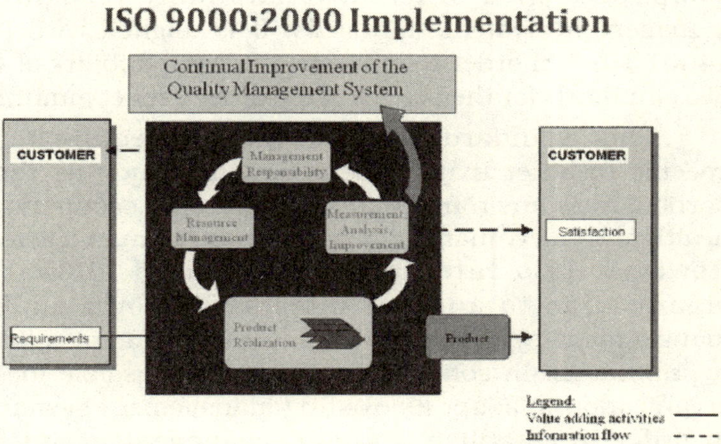

Fig. 5. ISO 9000:2000 - a process based approach

4.3.3.2. Relationship with ISO 9004

This edition of ISO 9001 has been developed as one part of a consistent pair of quality management system standards, the other being ISO 9000:2000 the two International Standards are designed to be used together, but can also be used independently. Although the two International Standards have different scopes, they have similar structures for ease of use.

This edition of ISO 9001 specifies requirements for a quality management system that may be used for internal application by organizations, certification, or contractual purposes.

ISO 9004:2000 gives guidance on a wider range of objectives of a quality management system to improve an organization's overall performance. ISO 9004:2000 is not a guideline for implementing ISO 9001:2000 and is not intended for certification or contractual use.

4.3.3.3. Compatibility with other management systems

This International Standard is intended to compatible with other internationally recognized management system standards. It is aligned with ISO 14001:1996 in order to enhance the compatibility of the two standards for the benefit of the other user community.

This Standard does not include requirements specific to other management systems, such as those particular to environmental management, occupational health and safety management, or financial management. However, this International Standard allows an organization to align or integrate its own quality management system with related management system requirements. In some cases, it may be possible for an organization to adapt its existing management system(s) in order to establish a quality management system complies with the requirements of this International Standard.

4.3.3.4. Structure of ISO 9001:2000

The structure of ISO 9000:2000 is as follows:

1. Scope
    a. General
    b. Permissible exclusions
2. Normative reference
3. Terms and definitions
4. Quality management system
    a. General requirements
    b. General documentation requirements
5. Management responsibility
    a. Management commitment
    b. Customer focus
    c. Quality policy
    d. Planning

e. Administration

f. Management review

6. Resource management

a. Provision of resources

b. Human resources

c. Facilities

d. Work environment

7. Product realization

a. Planning of realization process

b. Customer-related process

c. Design and/or development

d. Purchasing

e. Product and service operations

f. Control of measuring and monitoring devices

8. Measurement analysis and improvement

a. Planning

b. Measurement and monitoring

c. Control of nonconformity

d. Analysis of data

e. Improvement

4.4. CORRESPONDENCE BETWEEN ISO/DIS 9001:2000 AND ISO 9000:1994

Table 4 : Correspondence between ISO 9001:1994 and ISO/DIS 9001:2000

ISO 9001:1994	*ISO/DIS 9001:2000*
1 Scope	1
2 Normative reference	2
3 Definitions	3
4.1 Management responsibility	
4.1.1 Quality policy	5.1 + 5.3 + 5.4.1
4.1.2 Organization	5.5.2
4.1.2.1 Responsibility and authority	5.5.2 + 6.2.1

4.1.2.2 Resources	5.1 + 6.1 + 6.3
4.1.2.3 Management representative	5.5.3
4.1.3 Management review	5.6
4.2 Quality system	
4.2.1 General	4.x + 5.1 + 5.4.1 + 5.5.5
4.2.2 Quality system procedure	4.2
4.2.3 Quality planning	5.4.2 + 7.1
4.3 Contract review	7.2.2
4.4 Design control	7.3
4.5 Document and data control	5.5.6
4.6 Purchasing	7.4
4.7 Control of customer-supplied product	7.5.3
4.8 Product identification and traceability	7.5.2
4.9 Process control	7.1 + 7.5.1 + 7.5.5
4.10 Inspection and testing	7.1 + 7.5.1 + 8.1 + 8.2.4
4.11 Control of inspection, measuring and test equipment	7.6
4.12 Inspection and test status	7.5.1
4.13 Control of nonconforming product	8.3
4.14 Corrective and preventive action	8.4. + 8.5.2 + 8.5.3
4.15 Handling, storage, packaging, preservation and delivery	7.1 + 7.5.4
4.16 Control of quality records	5.5.7
4.17 Internal quality audit	8.2.2
4.18 Training	6.2.2
4.19 Servicing	7.1 + 7.5.1
4.20 Statistical techniques	8.1 + 8.2.3 + 8.2.4 +8.4

Table 5: Correspondence between ISO 9001:2000 and ISO 9001:1994

ISO/DIS 9001:2000	*ISO 9001:1994*
1 Scope	1
1.1 General	
1.2 Permissible exclusions	
2 Normative references	2
3 Terms and definitions	3
4 Quality management system	
4.1 General requirements	4.2.1

4.2 General documentation requirements	4.2.2
5 Management responsibility	
5.1 Management commitment	4.1 + 4.1.2.2 + 4.2.1
5.2 Customer focus	
5.3 Quality policy	4.1.1
5.4 Quality planning	
5.4.1 Quality Objectives	4.1.1 + 4.2.1
5.4.2 Quality planning	4.2.3
5.5 Administration	
5.5.1 General	
5.5.2 Responsibility and authority	4.1.2 + 4.1.2.1
5.5.3 Management representative	4.1.2.3
5.5.4 Internal communication	
5.5.5 Quality manual	4.2.1
5.5.6 Control of documents	4.5
5.5.7 Control of quality records	4.16
5.6 Management review	4.1.3
5.6.1 Review input	4.1.3
5.6.2 Review output	4.1.3
6 Resource management	4.1.2.2
6.1 Provision of resources	4.1.2.2
6.2 Human resources	
6.2.1 Assignment of personnel	4.1.2.1
6.2.2 Training, awareness and competency	4.18
6.3 Facility	4.9
6.4 Work environment	4.9
7 Product realization	
7.1 Planning of realization processes	4.2.3 + 4.9 + 4.10 + 4.15 + 4.19
7.2 Customer-related processes	
7.2.1 Identification of customer requirements	
7.2.2 Review of product requirements	4.3
7.2.3 Customer communication	
7.3 Design and/or development	4.4
7.3.1 Design and/or development planning	4.4.2. + 4.4.3
7.3.2 Design and/or development inputs	4.4.4
7.3.3 Design and/or development outputs	4.4.5
7.3.4 Design and/or development review	4.4.6
7.3.5 Design and/or development verification	4.4.7

7.3.6 Design and/or development validation	4.4.8
7.3.7 Control of design and/or development changes	4.4.9
7.4 Purchasing	
7.4.1 Purchasing control	4.6
7.4.2 Purchasing information	4.6
7.4.3 Verification of purchased product	4.6
7.5 Production and service operations	
7.5.1 Operations control	4.9 + 4.10 + 4.12 + 4.19
7.5.2 Identification and traceability	4.8
7.5.3 Customer supplied property	4.7
7.5.4 Preservation of product	4.15
7.5.5 Validation of processes	4.9
7.6 Control of measuring and monitoring devices	4.11
8 Measurement, analysis and improvement	
8.1 Planning	4.10 + 4.20
8.2 Measurement and monitoring	
8.2.1 Customer satisfaction	
8.2.2 Internal audit	4.17
8.2.3 Measurement and monitoring of processes	4.20
8.2.4 Measurement and monitoring of product	4.10 + 4.20
8.3 Control of nonconformity	4.13
8.4 Analysis of data	4.14 + 4.20
8.5 Improvement	
8.5.1 Planning for continual improvement	4.1.3 + 4.9
8.5.2 Corrective action	4.14
8.5.3 Preventive action	4.14

4.5. KEY CHANGES BETWEEN ISO 9001:1994 AND ISO 9001:2000

There are certain changes incorporated in the ISO 9001:2000. This revision has brought the flexibility and removed ambiguity of ISO 9001:1994.

4.5.1. Scope

ISO 9001:2000 - Clause 1.1 "General" : The scope has been enhanced by using the process approach addressing the requirements of customers i.e. customer satisfaction including the prevention of nonconformance.

ISO 9001:1994 - Clause 1 : The scope is to achieve the customer satisfaction through preventing nonconformance.

ISO 9001:2000 - Clause 1.2 "Permissible exclusions" : This is a new clause added to the International Standard.

ISO 9001:2000 permits organizations to exclude compliance with specific quality management system requirements that neither affect their ability nor absolve them from their responsibility, to provide product that meets customer and applicable regulatory requirements, yet still allows those organizations to claim conformity to the standard.

Permissible exclusions will be restricted to clause 7 Product realization of ISO 9001:2000 and will not apply to any other clauses of the standard.

4.5.2. Terms and Definitions

ISO 9001:2000 - Clause 3 "Terms and Definitions" : This clause states that the terms and definitions given in ISO 9000:2000 Quality management systems- Fundamentals and vocabulary, apply to ISO 9001:2000.

The term 'organization' used in ISO 9001:2000 replaces the term 'supplier', which was used previously to represent the unit to which ISO 9001 applied. The term 'supplier' is now used instead of the previous term 'subcontractor'. ISO 9001:2000 focuses on a new phrase "product realization", an abstract concept, which refers to the interconnected processes that are used to bring products into being. In short, from the inception of an idea to its ending up in the form of a product or service, this whole process is known as "product realization".

Fig. 6. Product Realization

ISO 9001:1994 - Clause 3 : The definitions that are given in ISO 8402 apply.

4.5.3. Management Responsibility

ISO 9001:2000 - Clause 5.1"Management commitment" : More emphasis is placed on Top Management commitment.

Particular attention should be given to sub-clauses (a), (b) and (e), the latter refers to resources and has a direct link to clause 6 "Resource Management".

a. communicating to the organization the importance of meeting customer as well as regulatory and legal requirements;

b. establishing the quality policy and the quality objectives;

c. conducting management reviews;

d. ensuring the availability of necessary resources

ISO 9001:1994 – Clauses 4.1; 4.1.2.2 and 4.2.1 are corresponding

The sub-clause a) is not explicitly stated.

ISO 9001:2000 - Clause 5.2 "Customer focus" : This is a completely new clause. It states that top management shall ensure that customer needs and expectations are determined and converted into requirements and fulfilled with the aim of achieving customer satisfaction.

There is no corresponding ISO 9001:1994 – Clause

ISO 9001:2000 - Clause 5.5.3 "Management Representative" : This clause says that Top management shall appoint member(s) of the management who, irrespective of other responsibilities, shall have defined authority that includes "promoting awareness of customer requirements throughout the organization".

ISO 9001:1994 - Clause 4.1.2.3 is corresponding

This version defines only one member from the organization as Management representative.

ISO 9001:2000 - Clause 5.5.4 "Internal Communication" : This is a new clause that requires the organization to ensure communication between the various levels and functions regarding the processes of the quality management system and their effectiveness.

There is no corresponding ISO 9001:1994 – Clause

ISO 9001:2000 - Clause 5.5.5 "Quality Manual": This clause has been enhanced to include the requirement for an organization to specify and justify any exclusion performed in the quality manual.

The quality manual shall also have a description of the sequence and interaction of the processes included in the quality management system

ISO 9001:1994 - Clause 4.2.1 is corresponding

This (ISO 9001 : 1994) International Standard series has three contractual standards as ISO 9001, ISO 9002 and ISO 9003 to support different sectors.

4.5.4. Product Realization

ISO 9001:2000 - Clause 7.2.1 "Identification of customer requirements" : Under this clause, two new requirements b) and c) have been added in the process of determining customers' needs.

a. product requirements specified by the customer, including the requirements for available, delivery and support:

b. product requirements not specified by the customer but necessary for intended or specified use;

c. obligations related to product, including regulatory and legal requirements.

There is no corresponding ISO 9001:1994 clause

ISO 9001:2000 - Clause 7.2.3 "Customer Communication" : This clause is essentially a new requirement, the organization is required to implement effective liaison with customers, with the aim of meeting customer requirements.

There is no corresponding ISO 9001:1994 Clause

4.5.5. Measurement, Analysis and Improvement

ISO 9001:2000 - Clause 8.2.1 "Customer satisfaction": This clause is new and emphasizes that the organization shall monitor and consider information on customer satisfaction and/or dissatisfaction as one of the measurement of performance of the quality management system.

There is no corresponding ISO 9001:1994 - Clause

The ISO 9000:2000 International Standard series is more flexible. It is an enhancement of ISO 9000:1994. It has removed several ambiguities of ISO 9000:1994 and a step towards the simplification. There is a shift in the approach to quality, as we know that ISO 9000:1994 emphasizes on "prevention nonconformance" while the ISO 9000:2000 emphasizes on checking the parameters of process like process characteristics and methodology.

4.6. ISO 9000 AND TOTAL QUALITY MANAGEMENT

Total Quality Management is a continuous process and a much broader concept than ISO 9000. However, we have tried to enlist some of their features in the Table 6.

Table 6 : Comparison between ISO 9000 and TQM

Standards	*ISO-9000*	*Total Quality Management*
Strategy for Quality	Inspection	Prevention
Basis	Based on standard procedures	Based on philosophy and concepts
Approach towards Continuous Improvement	Passive	Pro-active

Focus	Focused on set of procedures and design specifications, may or may not be focused on customer	Focused on Customer Satisfaction
Work Environment	Excessive Bureaucracy	Adhocratic
Scope	Narrow	Broad
Function	Majorly focused upon implementation of existing standard procedures and monitoring of functions	Focused on the improvement of existing standards and procedures.
Documentation	Based on strict documentation	No documentation is required
Flexibility	Lacks flexibility	Flexible, whenever required
Relationship with Suppliers	Controlled	Based on mutual trust, suppresses control
Workforce Development	Less Importance	Calls for extensive training of the staff
Workforce Participation	Less participation by employees	Emphasis on Employee participation
Impact on Operational Results	May not be significantly related	Positive impact

International Organization for Standardization has developed a series of standards for the Total Quality Management. These standards are provided for basically three types of organization:

1. ISO 9001: Quality systems-Model for quality assurance in design, development, production, installation and servicing

This whole model specifies all the requirements for use when conformance to specified requirements is to be assured during design, development, production, delivery and servicing. It provides the quality assurance model for demonstration by a supplier of its capability and for assessment by external parties. It is made up of twenty clauses.

2. ISO 9002: Quality system-Model for quality assurance in production, installation and servicing

This whole model specifies quality system requirements for use when installation conformance to specified requirements is to be assured by the supplier during production, installation and servicing. It provides a quality assurance model for demonstration of suppliers of its capability and for assessment of external parties.

3. ISO 9003: Quality system-Model for quality assurance in final inspection and test

This whole model specifies quality system requirements and it provides a model for the use where a supplier's capability is to be detected and controls the nonconformity during the final inspection and test.

4.7. WHY TQM THROUGH ISO 9000?

There are different approaches to TQM. It can be achieved through **Deming's** 14 points, **Juran's** triology, **Crosby's** Zero Defect, **Taguchi's** analytical approach or **Ishikawa's** method. These methods have their own pluses and minuses. ISO adapted the good points of all the methods and drafted it to a format which suits to manufacturing as well as services. It also provides consistency in the process. So, ISO 9000 is preferred over other methods in this project.

One most important way of implementation of TQM is implementing the ISO 9000 in the industry and service sectors. It provides the guidelines for use in any type of industry. It was developed by the **International Organization for Standardization**. It first appeared in the 1987, than it got updated in 1994 and was again revised in 2000. In this project, we will try to develop guidelines for implementing TQM in the libraries through ISO 9000 series of standards.

EXERCISES

1. Why a quality system is required for an organization?
2. What is Product standardization and role of ISO.
3. Write a note on ISO-9000.
4. Enumerate the changes between ISO 9000:1994 and ISO 9000:2000.
5. Give a descriptive account of structure of ISO9001:2000.
6. Discuss key changes between ISO 9001:1994 and ISO 9001:2000.
7. Differentiate between TQM and ISO 9000.

5

Quality Systems- Model for Quality Assurance in Design, Development, Production, Installation and Servicing

This chapter elaborates the requirements for Quality System by an organization planning to go for TQM implementation or ISO certification.

5.1. MANAGEMENT RESPONSIBILITY

5.1.1. Quality Policy

The supplier's management with executive responsibility shall define and document its policy for quality, including objectives for quality and its commitment to quality. The quality policy shall be relevant to the supplier's organizational goals and the expectations and needs of its customers. The supplier shall ensure that this policy is understood, implemented and maintained at all levels of the organization.

5.1.2. Organization

5.1.2.1. Responsibility and authority

The responsibility, authority and the interrelation of personnel who manages, performs and verifies work affecting quality shall be defined and documented, particularly for personnel who need the organizational freedom and authority to:

a) initiate action to prevent the occurrence of any non-conformities relating to product, process and quality system;

b) identify and record any problem relating to the product, process and quality system;

c) initiate, recommend or provide solutions through designated channels;

d) verify the implementation of solutions;

e) control further processing, delivery or installation of non-confirming product until the deficiency or unsatisfactory condition has been corrected.

5.1.2.2. Resources

The supplier shall identify resource requirements and provide adequate resources, including the assignment of trained personnel (see 4.18), for management, performance of work and verification activities including internal quality audits.

5.1.2.3. Management representative

The supplier's management with executive responsibility shall appoint a member of the supplier's own management who, irrespectively of other responsibilities, shall have defined authority for

a) ensuring that a quality system is established, implemented and maintained in accordance with this international standards, and

b) reporting on the performance of the quality system

to supplier's management for review and as a basis for improvement of the quality system.

Note 5 : The responsibility of management representative may also include liaison with external parties on matters relating to the supplier's quality system.

5.1.3. Management Review

The supplier's management with executive responsibility shall review the quality system at defined intervals sufficient to ensure its continuing suitability and effectiveness in satisfying the requirements of this International Standard and the supplier's stated quality policy and objectives (see 5.1.1). Record of such reviews shall be maintained (see 5.16).

Interpretation

1. The Top management must define Quality Policy. Quality Policy should be relevant and customer driven. It should define the factors, which can be measured during implementation. Communication of Quality Policy could be done by any method. Further, Quality Policy should be deployed to all the levels through the Quality Policy deployment.
2. The management should identify levels and positions in the organization through an organizational chart. Responsibilities and authorities for each of the position must be clearly defined. This chart must be able to show the line of hierarchy in the organization. Each personnel should be able to identify the problem, solution of problem within its authority. He/She should also have responsibility and authority to verify implementation of solution.
3. Resources should be reviewed and allocated in order to achieve the customer satisfaction.
4. Management should identify a responsible person

for the implementation of Quality System within the organization. He/She is the link between organization and Certifying body. He/She conducts internal quality audits and convenes management review meeting. He/She is also responsible for the implementation of Quality System.

5. Management Review should be according to fixed agenda. The agenda may be relevance of the quality policy, continuation of the resources, record of product non-conformities and concession, customer complaints and warranty claims, quality improvement plans, training and motivation of employees, any other quality related problems.

5.2. QUALITY SYSTEM

Scope : This clause establishes the need of Quality System by identifying the documented procedure through the quality planning.

5.2.1. General

The supplier shall establish, document and maintain a quality system as a means of ensuring that product conforms to specified requirements. The supplier shall prepare a quality manual covering the requirements of this International Standard. The quality manual shall include or make reference to the quality system procedures and outline the structure of the documentation used in the quality system.

Note 6 : Guidance on quality manuals is given in ISO 10013.

5.2.2. Quality System Procedure

The supplier shall

(a) prepare documented procedures consistent with the requirements of this International Standard and the supplier's stated Quality Policy, and

(b) effectively implement the quality system and its documented procedures

For the purpose of International Standard, range and the detail of the procedures that form part of the quality system shall be dependent upon the complexity of work, the method used, and the skills and training needed by personnel involved in carrying out the activity.

Note 7 : Documented procedures may make reference to work instructions that define how an activity is performed.

5.2.3. Quality Planning

Supplier shall define and document how the requirements for quality will be met. Quality planning shall be consistent with all other requirements of a supplier's quality system and shall be documented in a format to suit the supplier' method of operation. The supplier shall give consideration to the following activities, as appropriate, in meeting the specified requirements for products, projects or contracts:

a) the preparation of quality plans;

b) the identification and acquisition of any control, processes, equipment (including inspection and test equipment), fixtures resources and skills that may be needed to achieve the required quality;

c) ensuring the compatibility to the design, the production process, installation, servicing, inspection and test procedures and the applicable documentation;

d) the updating as necessary, of quality control, inspection and testing techniques, including development of new instrumentation;

e) the identification of any measurement requirement involving capability that exceeds the known states of art, in sufficient time of needed capability to developed;

f) the identification of suitable verification at appropriate stages in the realization of product;

g) the clarification of standards of acceptability for all features and requirements including those which contain a subjective element;

h) the identification and preparation of quality records (see 5.16)

Note 8: The quality plans referred to [see 5.2.3 a] may be in the form of a reference to the appropriate documented procedures that form and integral part of the supplier's quality system.

Interpretation

1. A Quality manual should be preferred. Manual should define all the procedures required to be done in order to do the job or if some guideline is given for the procedure a reference should be made to that document. ISO 10013 gives guidelines for Quality Manual.
2. The development of all three levels of documents should taken place by involving all the concerned under the consultant of Management Representative. Number of controlled copies must be defined (See Figure 7).
3. Documented procedure should be prepared for each of the activity and to implement it. The procedure can be defined itself or a reference can be made.
4. Quality plan should be drafted in detail as, what and when should be done, who should do it and how to perform a task keeping the customer satisfaction in mind.

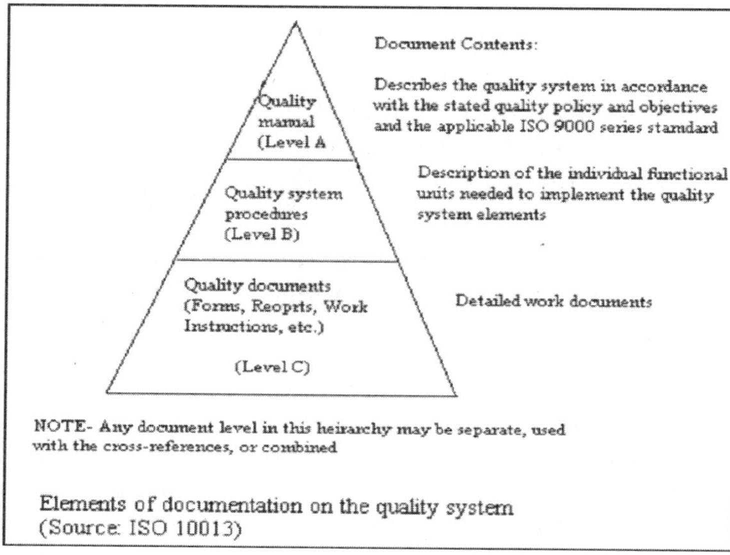

Fig. 7. Elements of Documentation on the Quality System (Source Courtesy ISO 10013)

5.3. CONTRACT REVIEW

Scope : This clause explains how to review the contracts and its use for Quality system implementation.

5.3.1. General

The supplier shall establish and maintain documented procedures for contract review and for the coordination of these activities.

5.3.2. Review

Before submission of a tender, or the acceptance of a contract or order (statement of requirement), the tender, contract or order shall be reviewed by the supplier to ensure that:

a) the requirements are adequately defined and documented; where no written statement of requirement is available for an order received by verbal means, the supplier shall ensure that the order requirements are agreed before their acceptance:

b) any differences between the contract or order requirements and those in the tender are resolved;

c) the supplier has the capability to meet the contract or order requirements.

5.3.3. Amendment to a contract

The supplier shall identify how an amendment to a contract is made and correctly transferred to the functions concerned within the supplier's organization.

5.3.4. Records

Records of contract reviews shall be maintained (see 5.16).

Note 9 : Channels for communication and interfaces with the customer's organization in these contract matters should be established.

Interpretation

1. A documented procedure should be established for the review of contracts.
2. Organization must review contract with customer. Procedure for the amendment must be drafted. Amendment must be known to all concerned departments.
3. Records of all the amendments must be kept.

5.4. DESIGN CONTROL

Scope : It is basically required in the organizations which are indulged in designing of product. Since, library is a service organization so this clause is not applicable as such but it needs this clause in designing of services.

5.4.1. General

The supplier shall establish and maintain

documented procedures to control and verify the design of the product in order to ensure that the specified requirements are met.

5.4.2. Design and development planning

The supplier shall prepare plans for each design and development activity. The plans shall describe or reference these activities, and define responsibility for there implementation. The design and development activities shall be assigned to qualified personnel equipped with adequate resources. The plan shall be updated as the design evolves.

5.4.3. Organizational and technical interface

Organizational and technical interfaces between different groups, which input into the design process shall be defined and the necessary information documented, transmitted and regularly reviewed.

5.4.4. Design input

Design input requirements related to the product, including applicable statutory and regulatory requirements, shall be identified, documented and their selection reviewed by the supplier for adequacy. Incomplete, ambiguous or conflicting requirements shall be resolved with those responsible for imposing these requirements.

Design input shall take into consideration the results of any contract review activity.

5.4.5. Design output

Design output shall be documented and expressed in terms that can be verified and validated against design input requirements.

Design output shall:

a) meet the design input requirements;

b) contain or make reference to acceptance criteria;

c) identify those characteristics of the design that are crucial to safe and proper functioning of the product (e.g. operating, storage, handling, maintenance and disposal requirements).

Design output shall be reviewed before release.

5.4.6. Design review

At appropriate stages of design, formal documented reviews of the design results shall be planned and conducted. Participants at each design review shall include representatives of all functions concerned with the design stage being reviewed, as well as other specialist personnel, as required. Records of such reviews shall be maintained (see 5.16).

5.4.7. Design verification

At appropriate stages of design verification shall be performed to ensure that the design stage output meets the design stage input requirements. The design verification measures shall be recorded (see 5.16).

Note 10 : In addition to conducting design reviews, design verification may include activities such as

- performing alternative calculations,
- comparing the new design with the similar proven design, if available,
- undertaking tests and demonstrations, and
- reviewing the design stage documents before release.

5.4.8. Design validation

Design validation shall be performed to ensure that product conforms to defined user needs and/or requirements.

Notes

11 Design validation follows successful design verification (see 5.4.7).

12 Validation is normally performed under defined operating conditions.

13 Validation is normally performed on final product, but may be necessary in earlier stages prior to product completion.

14 Multiple validations may be performed if there are different intended uses.

5.4.9. Design Changes

All design changes and modifications shall be identified, documented, reviewed and approved by authorized personnel before their implementation.

Interpretation

1. Overall the organization should have a documented procedure for control and maintenance of design for the customer satisfaction.
2. In order to design the product according to customer's demand a list of customer's requirement should be maintained so that in future product can be reviewed in light of the requirements.
3. Plan for each product or service, should be designed by a qualified person. The plan should include all the steps of the activities and individual responsibility. Any change in design should lead to change the plan accordingly.
4. Interface for both internal customers (organizational) and input for the process (technical) should be well defined. The information regarding the design should be communicated to all the concerned units.
5. Document the design input requirements. Design input should be chosen under the consideration of statutory and regulatory, contract reviews etc. requirements. Any ambiguity in the requirements for design must be sorted out.
6. A periodical review of the different stages of product

design should be done. Reviewing body should consist of representatives of all concerned departments.

7. The purpose of carrying out design verification activities is to ensure that the design output meets the design input requirements in terms of measurable units. The design verification can be done by any one, or more, of the following methods:
   a) Design review- This must be done by agencies other than those who developed the design.
   b) Alternate calculations.
   c) Prototype testing.
   d) Comparing with a similar proven design.
8. Design validation can be done once the product is made. It is to be checked to what extent the product is meeting the customer's requirements. If product has multiple uses it can also be tested under different environments.
9. Design change should be known and approved by the competent authority. The change in the design must be drafted and documented. And the earlier design must be stored explaining the appropriate need of change.

5.5. DOCUMENT AND DATA CONTROL

Scope : Control of all data and documents related to the standards is covered in this clause.

5.5.1. General

The supplier shall establish and maintain documented procedures to control all documents and data that relate to the requirements of this International Standard including, to the extent applicable, documents of external origin such as standards and customer drawings.

Notes 15 : Documents and data can be in the form of any type of media, such as hard copy or electronic media.

5.5.2. Document and data approval and issue

The documents and the data shall be reviewed and approved for adequacy by authorized personnel prior to issue. A master list or equivalent document control procedure identifying the current revision status of documents should be established and be readily available to preclude the use of invalid and/or obsolete documents.

This control shall ensure that:

a) the pertinent issues of appropriate documents are available at all locations where operations essential to the effective functioning of the quality system are performed;

b) invalid and/or obsolete documents are promptly removed from all points of issue or use, or otherwise assured against unintended use;

c) any obsolete documents retained for legal and/or knowledge-preservation purposes are suitably identified.

5.5.3. Document and data changed

Changes of the document and data shall be reviewed and approved by the same functions/organizations that performed the original review and approval, unless specifically designated otherwise. The designated functions/organization shall have access to pertinent background information upon which to base their review and approval.

Where practicable, the nature of the change shall be identified in the document or the appropriate attachments.

Interpretation

1. Organization should identify the different categories of quality related documents and should store it separately. For example, Quality guidelines documents, Documents of external origin, Documents of internal origin, or Miscellaneous documents.
2. A Master document should have entry of all the documents under control. The master document should contain latest version of the quality documents, number of copies, location number and current status. The obsolete documents should be immediately removed and kept for the archival purpose.
3. There should have a authority which should approve the quality records. Authority and responsibility for approval, issue and review of documents should be clearly defined. If the documents are stored in soft copy proper backup should be made access to it should be highly restricted.
4. The manual can be stored in the hard disk as well as hard copy depending on the choice the organization.

5.6. PURCHASING

Scope : This clause explains the purchasing procedure and its need in organization.

5.6.1. General

The supplier shall establish and maintain documented procedures to ensure that purchased product conforms to specified requirements.

5.6.2. Evaluation of sub-contractors

The supplier shall:

a) evaluation and select subcontractors on the basis of their ability to meet subcontract requirements including the quality system and any specific quality assurance requirements;

b) define the type and extent of control exercised by the supplier over subcontractors. This shall be dependent upon the type of product, the impact of subcontracted product on the quality audit reports and/or quality records of the previously demonstrated capability and performance of subcontractors;

c) establish and maintain quality records of acceptable subcontractors (see 5.16).

5.6.3. Purchasing data

Purchasing documents shall contain data clearly describing the product ordered, including where applicable:

a) the type class, grade or other precise identification;

b) the title or other positive identification, and applicable issues of specifications, drawing, process requirements, inspection instructions and other relevant technical data, including requirements for approval or qualification of product, procedures, process equipment and personnel;

c) the title, number and issue of the quality system standard to be applied.

The supplier shall review and approve purchasing documents for the adequacy of the specified requirements prior to release.

5.6.4. Verification of purchased product

5.6.4.1. Supplier's verification at sub-contractors premises

Where the supplier proposes to verify purchased product at the sub-contractor's premises, the supplier shall specify verification arrangements and the method of product release in the purchasing documents.

5.6.4.2. Customer verification of subcontracted product

Where specified in the contract, the supplier's customer or the customer's representative shall be afforded the right to verify at the subcontractor's premises that subcontracted product confirms to specified requirements. Such verification shall not be used by the supplier as evidence of effective control of quality by the subcontractor.

Verification by the customer shall not absolve the supplier of the responsibility to provide acceptable product, nor shall it prelude subsequent rejection by the customer.

Interpretation

1. Documented procedure should be made for purchase like placing the order, reviewing product, accepting the invoices etc.
2. A documented list of accepted sub-contractors should be maintained. Sub-contractors should be accepted when they qualify the laid quality requirements by the organization. Thus accepted sub-contractors should identified and listed. A periodic review of Sub-contractor should be done on the basis of their performance of the past days and a report should be made. One copy of the report should also send to sub-contractor.
3. The Purchase Document should have the all the necessary specifications including type, grade, design and identification of the product. A competent authority in the organization should review the purchase document before sending it for order.
4. Organization should maintain procedure for verifying product at the sub-contractors premises. Organization should arrange the audit at the sub-contractor's premises.

5. Organization should maintain procedure for verification by its customers at sub-contractor's premises, in contract itself, if it is necessary for the customers satisfaction.

5.7. CONTROL OF CUSTOMER-SUPPLIED PRODUCT

Scope : This clause provides guidelines for organization, how to handle products, provided by the customer.

The supplier shall establish and maintain documented procedures for the control of verification, storage and maintenance of customer-supplied product provided for incorporation into the supplies or for related activities. Any such product that is lost, damaged or is otherwise unsuitable for use shall be recorded and reported to the customer (see 4.16).

Verification by the supplier does not absolve the customer of the responsibility to provide accepted product.

Interpretation

Any product of customer sent in order to incorporate in the final product should be identified separately, verified, documented. It should be clearly documented how to handle the product during the process. Any nonconformity found in such a product should be recorded and immediately brought into the consideration of customer.

5.8. PRODUCT IDENTIFICATION AND TRACEABILITY

Scope : This clause provides guidelines to identify any product used inside process as well as outside the process and whenever it is required it can be traced immediately.

Where appropriate, the supplier shall establish and maintain documented procedures for identifying the product by suitable means from receipt and during all stages of production, delivery and installation.

Where and to the extent that traceability is a specified requirement, the supplier shall establish and maintain documented procedures for unique identification of individual product or batches. This identification shall be recorded (see 5.16).

Interpretation

There should be a proper method to identify the products. For that each product should be given some name or tag, individually or group depending on the condition. The system should be such that it should provide for tracing product when it is necessary.

5.9. PROCESS CONTROL

Scope : This clause includes all operational activities of library and guides how to perform individual activity.

The supplier shall identify and plan the production, installation and servicing which directly affects quality and shall ensure that these processes are carried out under control conditions shall include the following:

a) documented procedure defining the manner of production, installation and servicing, where the absence of such procedure could adversely affect quality;

b) use of suitable production, installation and servicing equipment, and a suitable working environment;

c) compliance with reference standards/codes, quality plans and/or documented procedures;

d) monitoring and control of suitable process parameters and product characteristics;

e) the approval of the processes and equipment, as appropriate;

f) criteria for workmanship, which shall be stipulated in the clearest practical manner (e.g. written standards, representative samples or illustrations);

g) suitable maintenance of equipment to ensure continuing process capability.

Where the result of processes cannot be fully verified by subsequent inspection and testing of the product where, for example, processing deficiencies may become apparent only after the product is in use, the processes shall be carried out by qualified operators and/or shall require continuous monitoring and control of process parameters to ensure that the specified requirements are met.

The requirements for any qualification of process operations, include associated equipment and personnel (see 5.18) shall be specified.

Note 11 : Such processes requiring pre-qualification of their process capability are frequently referred to as special processes.

Records shall be maintained for qualified processes, equipment and personnel, as appropriate (see 5.16).

Interpretation

Critical process should be identified. Characteristics of such process should be identified. Monitoring of such process must be done particularly those products, which cannot be tested unless it goes to the hand of customers. Equipment used in the process must be the standardized and calibrated. Procedures discussed above must be documented to provide guide to the workers.

5.10. INSPECTION AND TESTING

Scope : This clause includes the specifications for the inspection and testing of the procedures, incoming material and of final product.

5.10.1. General

The supplier shall establish and maintain documented procedures for inspection and testing activities in order to verify that the specified requirements for the product are met. The required inspection and testing, and the record to be established, shall be detailed in the quality plan or documented procedures.

5.10.2. Receiving inspection and testing

The supplier shall ensure that incoming product is not used or processed (except in the circumstances described in 5.10.2.3) until it has been inspected or otherwise verified as confirming to specified requirements. Verification of conformance to the specified requirements shall be in accordance with the quality plan and/or documented procedures.

In determining the amount and nature of receiving inspection, consideration shall be given to the amount of control exercised at the subcontractor's premises and the recorded evidence of conformance provided.

Where in coming product is released for urgent production purposes prior to verification, it shall be positively identified and recorded (5.16) in order to permit immediate recall and replacement in the event of nonconformity to specified requirements.

5.10.3. In-process inspection and testing

The supplier shall:

a) inspect and test the product as required by the quality plan and/or documented procedures;

b) hold product until the required inspection and tests have been completed or necessary reports have been received and verified, except when product is released under positive recall procedures (see 5.10.2.3). Release under positive-recall procedures shall not preclude the activities outlined in 5.10.3 a).

5.10.4. Final inspection and testing

The supplier shall carry out all final inspection and testing in accordance with quality plan and/or documented procedure to complete the evidence of conformance of the finished product to the specified requirements.

The quality plan and/or documented procedures for final inspection and testing shall required that all specified inspection and tests, including those specified either on receipt of the product or in-process, have been carried out and that the results meet specified requirements.

No product shall be dispatched until all the activities specified in the quality plan and/or documented procedures have been satisfactorily completed and the associated data and documentation are available and authorized.

5.10.5. Inspection and test records

The supplier shall establish and maintain records, which provide evidence that the product has been inspected and/or tested. These records shall show clearly whether the product has passed or failed the inspections and/or tests according to defined acceptance criteria. Where the product fails to pass any inspection and/or test, the procedures for control of nonconforming product shall apply (see 5.13).

Record shall identify the inspection authority responsible for the release of product (see 5.16).

Interpretation

Documented procedure for inspection and testing should be established in the quality plan of organization keeping the customer satisfaction in mind.

Received materials should be inspected before the actual use in organization. It should be done according to the contract made between the organization and it's supplier. Products should also be inspected during the process at different stages.

If in any case there is an urgent need for the material in process, a received material can be installed without any inspection and test but such material should be specially identified and recorded.

The organization should also determine considerable amount of control on subcontractor by periodical review of product and process at the subcontractor's premises if such a contract is already made.

Reports should be generated out of the different levels of inspection. All the reports should be submitted at the time of finally inspection of product. All the inspected products or services must be delivered to the customers.

Reports should be recorded irrespective to the product's conformance and nonconformance. The name of the inspecting authority must be mentioned on the report.

5.11. CONTROL OF INSPECTION, MEASURING AND TEST EQUIPMENT

Scope : Clause explains control and calibration procedure for the test equipments.

5.11.1. General

The supplier shall establish and maintain documented procedures to control, calibrate and maintain inspection, measuring and test equipment (including test software) used by the supplier to demonstrate the conformance of product to the specified requirements. Inspection, measuring and test equipment shall be used in a manner which, ensures that the measurement uncertainty is known and is consistent with the required measurement capability.

Where test software or comparative references such as test hardware are used as suitable forms of inspection, they shall be checked to prove that they are capable of verifying the acceptability of product, prior to release for use during production, installation or servicing, and shall be rechecked at prescribed intervals. The supplier shall establish the extent and frequency of such checks and shall maintain records as evidence of control (see 5.16).

Where the availability of technical data pertaining to the inspection, measuring and test equipment is a specified requirement, such data shall be made available, when required by the customer of customer's representative, for verification that the inspection, measuring and test equipment is functionally adequate.

Note 17 : For the purpose of this International Standard the term "Measuring Equipment" includes measurement devices.

5.11.2. Control Procedure

The supplier shall:

a) determine the measurement to be made and the accuracy required, and select the appropriate inspection, measuring and test equipment that is capable of the necessary accuracy and precision;

b) identify all inspection, measuring and test equipment that can affect product quality, and calibrate and adjust them at prescribed intervals, or prior to use, against certified equipment having a known valid relationship to internationally or nationally recognized standards. Where no such standards exist, the basis used for calibration shall be documented;

c) define the process employed for the calibration of inspection, measuring and test equipment, including details of equipment type, unique identification, location, frequency of checks, check method, acceptance criteria and the action to be taken when results are unsatisfactory;

d) identify inspection measuring and test equipment with a suitable indicator or approved identification record to show the calibration status;

e) maintain calibration records for inspection, measuring and test equipment (see 4.16);

f) assess and document the validity of previous inspection and test results when inspection, measuring and test equipment is found to be out of calibration;

g) ensure that governmental conditions are suitable for the calibrations, inspection measurements and tests being carried out;

h) ensure that the handling, preservation and storage of inspection, measuring and test equipment is such that the accuracy and fitness for use are maintained;

i) safeguard inspection, measuring and test facility, including both test hardware and test software, form adjustments which would invalidate the calibration setting.

Note 18 : The metrological confirmation system for measuring equipment is given in ISO 10012 may be used for guidance.

Interpretation

Periodical calibration of test equipment should be organized to find out their conformity or to identify the degree of uncertainty in the measurement. A documented procedure should be made to perform such verification. So it is necessary to maintain the calibration records.

The degree of acceptance should be identified for each of the test equipment. If it is out of calibration, the eariier calibration process should be checked. The calibration instruments should be kept in the controlled condition.

5.12. INSPECTION AND TEST STATUS

Scope : Inspection and test status has application to identify conformity and nonconformity of product.

The inspection and test status of product shall be identified by suitable means, which indicates the conformance of product with regard to inspection and test performed. The identification of inspection and test shall be maintained, as defined in the quality plan and/ or documented procedures, through out production, installation and servicing of the product to ensure that only product that has passed the required inspection and test [or released under the authorized concession (see 5.13.2)] is dispatched, used or installed.

Interpretation

Form receipt to dispatch, all the products should be uniequally, identified to know their status for the products under inspection, waiting for inspection, rejected etc.

5.13. CONTROL OF NONCONFORMING PRODUCTS

Scope : Nonconforming products should be controlled.

5.13.1. General

The supplier shall establish and maintain documented procedures to ensure that product that does not conform to specified requirements is prevented from unintended use or installation. This control shall provide for identification, documentation, evaluation, segregation (when practical), disposition of nonconforming product, and for notification to functions concerned.

5.13.2. Review and Disposition of Nonconforming Product

The responsibility for review and authority for the disposition of nonconforming product shall be defined.

Nonconforming product shall be reviewed in accordance with documented procedures. It may be

a) reworked to meet the specified requirements,

b) accepted with or without repair by concession,

c) regarded for alternative applications, or

d) rejected on scrapped.

Where required by the contract, the proposed use or repair of product [see 5.13.2 b)] which does not conforms to specified requirements shall be reported for concession to the customer or customer's representative. The description of the nonconformity that has been accepted, and of repairs, shall be recorded to denote the actual condition (see 5.16).

Repaired and/or reworked product shall be re-inspected in accordance with the quality plan and/or documented procedures.

Interpretation

Nonconforming product should be identified and documented through the verification of products. Such product should be separated from the lot of the conformed product and a program should be laid down to get ride of such product.

The method of disposition should be defined. If it is within a limit of acceptance the product can be accepted or it can be disposed by providing customer relaxation in the price or by any means. If it is not at all acceptable it can be sent for rework and after rework it must be reviewed as defined in the quality plan.

5.14. CORRECTIVE AND PREVENTIVE ACTION

Scope : All corrective measured must be taken care during the design, production, installation and servicing.

5.14.1. General

The supplier shall establish and maintain

documented procedures for implementing corrective and preventive action.

Any corrective or preventive action taken to eliminate the causes of actual or potential non-conformities shall be to a degree appropriate to the magnitude of problems and commensurate with the risks encountered.

The supplier shall implement and record any changes to the documented procedures resulting form corrective and preventive action.

5.14.2. Corrective action

The procedure for corrective action shall include:

a) the effective handling of customer complaints and reports of product non-conformities;

b) investigation of cause of non-conformities relating to product, process and quality system, and recording the results of the investigation (see 5.16);

c) determination of the corrective action needed to eliminate the cause of non-conformities;

d) application of controls to ensure that corrective action is taken it is effective.

5.14.3. Preventive action

The procedures for preventive action shall include-

a) the use of appropriate sources of information such as processes and work operations which affect product quality, concessions, audit results, quality records, service reports and customer complaints to detect, analyze and eliminate potential causes of non-conformities;

b) determination of the steps needed to deal with any problems requiring preventive action;

c) initiation of preventive action and application of controls to ensure that it is effective;

d) ensuring that relevant information on actions taken is submitted for management review (see 5.1.3).

Interpretation

Correction and prevention should be done whenever and wherever non-conformity is seen. For implementing corrective and preventive actions, procedure should be documented. If any preventive action or corrective action brings out some change in product or process it should be recorded.

5.15. HANDLING, STORAGE, PACKAGING, PRESERVATION AND DELIVERY

Scope : This clause enunciates handling, storage, packaging, preservation and delivery of product.

5.15.1. General

The supplier shall establish and maintain documented procedures for handling, storage, packaging, preservation and delivery of product.

5.15.2. Handling

The supplier shall provide methods of handling product that prevent damage or deterioration.

5.15.3. Storage

The supplier shall use designated storage areas or stock rooms to prevent damage or deterioration of product, pending use or delivery. Appropriate methods for authorizing receipt to and dispatch from such areas shall be stipulated.

In order to detect deterioration, the condition of product in stock shall be assessed at appropriate intervals.

5.15.4. Packaging

The supplier shall control packing, packaging and marking processes (including materials used) to the extent necessary to ensure conformance to specified requirements.

5.15.5. Preservation

The supplier shall apply appropriate methods for preservation of product when the product is under the supplier's control.

5.15.6. Delivery

The supplier shall arrange for the protection of the quality of product after final inspection and test. Where contractually specified, this protection shall be extended to include delivery to destination.

Interpretation

1. Procedures for handling, storage, packaging, preservation and delivery should be drafted.
2. Try to minimize damage of the product due improper handling method. One should provide guidelines how to handle the product during process or transportation.
3. There should be proper storage area at the supplier's place to store the product or inventories. Periodic review should be done to identify the level of deterioration of product or inventories. The level of deterioration should be documented.
4. Product should be packed and marked such that it should show that it is in conformance with specific requirement.
5. The organization must take care for preservation of products and inventories.
6. Organization must ensure the protection of product during the transportation. And where it is contractually specified it must take care of product upto delivery.

5.16. CONTROL OF QUALITY RECORDS

Scope : Quality records should be stored in such a way that it is easy to retrieve whenever and wherever it is required.

The supplier shall establish and maintain documented procedures for identification, collection, indexing, access, filing, storage, maintenance and disposition of quality records.

Quality records shall be maintained to demonstrate conformance to specified requirements and the effective operation of the quality system. Pertaining quality records from the subcontractor shall be an element of these data.

All quality records shall be legible and shall be stored and retained in such a way that they are readily retrievable in facilities that provide a suitable environment to prevent damage or deterioration and to prevent loss. Retention times of quality records shall be established and recorded. Where agreed contractually, quality records shall made available for evaluation by the customer or the customer's representative for an agreed period.

Note 19 : Records may be in the form of any type of media, such as hard copy or electronic media.

Interpretation

Quality records are outcome of the process in order to show the conformance of product. These records must be stored, indexed and filed in such a way that their retrieval become easy whenever it is needed. For each record a retention time should be recorded. It can be stored in any type of medium.

5.17. INTERNAL QUALITY AUDIT

Scope : This clause explains how to conduct internal quality audit in the organization.

The supplier shall establish and maintain documented procedures for planning and implementing internal quality audits to verify whether quality activities and related results comply with planned arrangements and to determine the effectiveness of the quality system.

Internal quality audits shall be scheduled on the basis of the status and importance of the activity to be audited and shall be carried out by personnel independent of those having direct responsibility for the activity being audited.

The results of the audits shall be recorded (see 5.16) and brought to the attention of the personnel having responsibility in the area audited. The management personnel responsible for the area shall take timely corrective action on deficiencies found during the audit.

Follow-up audit activities shall verify and record the implementation and effectiveness of the corrective action taken (see 5.16).

Note 20 : The results of internal quality audits from an integral part of the input to management review activities (see 5.1.3).

Note 21 : The guidance on quality system audits is given in ISO 10011.

Interpretation

The concerned organization should conduct Internal quality audit to check the performance of the organization. It should be carried out at different intervals and the frequency must be determined according to the importance of the work. The procedure to conduct such audits must be documented. Findings of such audit must be recorded and presented for quality review. Any irregularity must be recorded and brought in the consideration of concerned authority.

5.18. TRAINING

Scope : Impart skill among the workers in the organization.

The supplier shall establish and maintain documented procedures for identifying training needs and provide for the training of all personnel performing activities affecting quality. Personnel performing specific assigned task shall be qualified of the basis of appropriate education, training and/or experience, as required. Appropriate records of training shall be maintained (see 5.16).

Interpretation

Organization should work to upgrade skills of employees. It should conduct time to time seminars, workshop or training programs for upgrading. Procedure for training should be documented for the different levels of workers.

5.19. SERVICING

Scope : Servicing after the sales.

Where servicing is a specified requirement, the supplier shall establish and maintain documented procedure for performing, verifying and reporting that the servicing meets the specified requirements.

Interpretation

If the supplier has the contract to provide service after the sale of product there should be a procedural draft for providing service.

5.20. STATISTICAL TECHNIQUES

5.20.1. Identification of need

The supplier shall identify the need for statistical techniques required for establishing, controlling and verifying process capability and product characteristics.

5.20.2. Procedure

The supplier shall establish and maintain documented procedures to implement and control the application of the statistical techniques identified in 5.20.1.

Interpretation

Organization should identify the various statistical techniques for implementation of the quality system.

The organization should identify the documented procedure for statistical techniques. Organization can use any one of following tools:

i. Check sheet

ii. Pareto analysis

iii. Histogram

iv. Cause-and-effect diagram

v. Stratification

vi. Scatter diagram

vii. Graph and control charts.

EXERCISES

1. Enumerate various clauses (based on ISO 9000:1994) that will be taken into consideration to establish a quality system.
2. Discuss the role of inspection in the quality system.
3. Discuss Management Responsibility in the successful implementation of Quality System.

6
ISO 9000 Implementation in Libraries

Libraries are service organization. Basically it is understood that libraries are depository for books. The motto of library services is to provide "Right information to the Right person at the Right time" and "Best information for the *largest* number at the *least* cost". In order to fulfill these motto libraries provide a variety of services to the users associated with the library. Such services may range from issuing a book to providing exact information demanded from the user. Libraries can offer circulation of books, documentation service like current awareness service, reprographic service. Besides these services, libraries can support other libraries or share resources of other libraries through the resource sharing.

6.1. QUALITY IN LIBRARY

According to ISO 8402 'Quality Assurance and quality control vocabulary' the term Quality means:

"Totality of characteristic of an entity that bears on its ability to satisfy stated and implied need."

The features and characteristics appeared in manufacturing as well as service sectors are same for library, so ISO 9000 is also applicable for library.

6.2. WHICH STANDARD IS APPLICABLE?

ISO 9000 has three contractual standards, ISO 9001, ISO 9002 and ISO 9003. ISO 9003 is only for the organizations which are involved in Inspection and Testing. ISO 9001 is for those organizations, which are involved in Designing products. Such organizations are mostly involved in R & D for example NASA (In U. S.), ISRO (In India), General Motors, Fords etc.

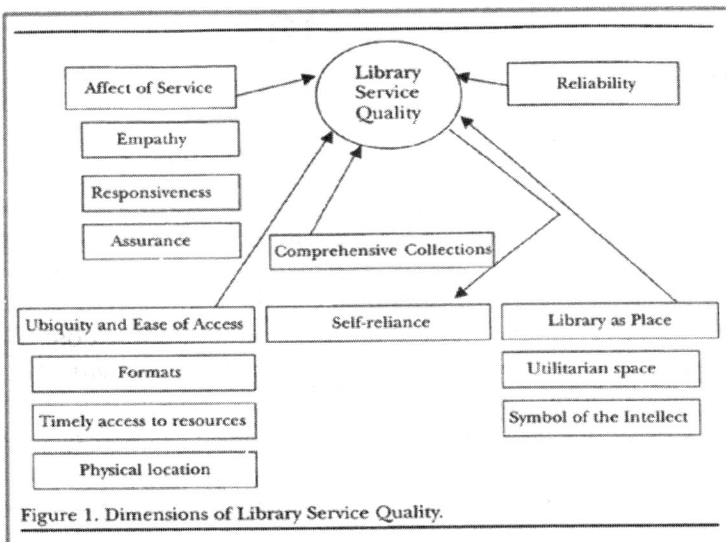

Fig. 8. Dimensions of Library Service Quality.
(Source Courtesy: http://www.libqual.org/documents/admin/cookheath.pdf)

It is also applicable for the service sectors like hospitals, banks, catering, entertainment, distributors, stockists, insurance-corporation, professionals like lawyers, consultant, training and education. Similarly libraries are also service providers but not involved in the designing of any physical product. So, in libraries ISO 9002 is applicable.

Application of ISO 9002 Clauses

There are nineteen clauses in ISO 9002. Except 5.4 i.e. 'Design control' all clauses are applicable.

Requirements for Quality System for a library are detailed below:

6.3. MANAGEMENT RESPONSIBILITY

i. Management must define a Quality policy and implement it in the organization.

ii. There should be an organizational chart.

   1. Responsibility and authority should be defined.
   2. Resources should be identified and adequately allocated.
   3. Management should identify a Management representative.

iii. Periodical review should be done by Management review committee.

Recommendations

1. The Top management (generally referred as Library council/Library committee) of library must define a Quality Policy. Quality Policy should be relevant and 'User' driven. It should define the factors which can be measured during implementation.

   There can be many Quality Policy statements. One of the best Quality Policy statements can be the 'Five laws of Library Science' which was restated by Prof. G. Bhattacharya as:

   A. Information is for use,

   B. Every user his/her information,

   C. Every information its user,

   D. Save the time of user,

E. Library/information centre is a growing organism.

All the statements are measurable. For example, if library has some information, which is not been ever used then one can measure quantitatively how much waste information is there in library. Similarly, one can quantify how many users are not getting the relevant information and how much time it is taking to give a service to a user. Finally, one can measure how much growth is there in library in the terms of resources and users [Figure 9].

Communication of Quality Policy could be done by any method. One of the trusted ways is to post it at convenient places in the library.

Quality Policy should be deployed to all the levels through the Quality Policy deployment.

2. The Library management committee should identify levels and positions in the library through an organizational chart. Responsibilities and authorities for each of the position must be clearly defined. This chart must able to show the line of hierarchy in the organization. Each personnel should be able to identify the problem, solution of problem within his/her authority. He/She should also have responsibility and authority to verify implementation of solution.

3. Resources like human resource, finance, state-of-the-art technology etc. should be identified and allocated in order to achieve the maximum level of customer satisfaction.

4. Library management should identify a responsible person for the implementation of Quality System within the library as the Management Representative. He/She is the link between organization and Certifying-body. He/She conducts internal quality audits and convenes management

review meeting. He/She is also responsible for the implementation of Quality System in the library. The suited person for Management Representative in the library can be the Chief librarian or the Deputy-librarian.

5. There should be Management Review according to fixed agenda. The Reviewing committee should consist of Management Representative, Heads of the different sections and President of the Management committee and members of the Management Committee. The periodicity of such review can be defined by Management Committee. This committee is a place for the discussion and decision-making according to the following agenda:

   A. Performance review in the light of policy deployment.
   B. Relevance of the Quality Policy,
   C. Review of resources,
   D. User complaints and concessions,
   E. Quality improvement planes,
   F. Training and motivation of employees, &
   G. Any other quality related problems.

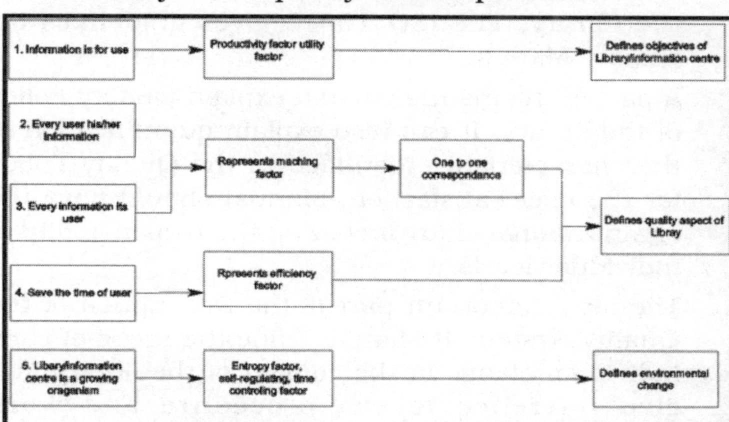

Fig. 9. Five Laws as Quality Policy

All the decisions, observations and conclusions taken by the Management Review Committee must be recorded and followed up by the Management Representative.

Quality System

a. The supplier shall establish, document and maintain a quality system as a means of ensuring that product conforms to specified requirements.

b. Supplier should lay down documented procedures consistent with requirements of ISO 9000.

c. Supplier shall state the Quality policy in its Quality Assurance Manual.

d. Supplier shall lay down Quality plan.

Recommendations

Three or four levels of documentation can be done in the library.

A. First level: Quality Assurance Manual

i. The introductory pages of the manual should contain the title and scope of the manual. Few introductory pages should give the brief account of the library. The ISO 10013 gives guidelines for Quality Manual.

ii. A part of the manual should explain Quality Policy of the library. It can also explain quantification of the characteristics identified in the Quality Policy for the user satisfaction. Manual should have the organizational chart including the responsibility of individual levels.

iii. The most important part is the Description of the Quality System. It should define the scope of each individual clause in the context of the library and give reference to the procedure and work instruction.

B. Second level: Quality System Procedure:

The Quality System Procedure and Work instruction are almost same except that work instructions are operating instruction for performing a specific job, and gives guidance how a specific job can be performed. These instructions and procedures are documented in a separate document called and Quality Procedure Manual. All the procedures of library should be documented step by step in the Procedure Manual.

C. Third level : Forms and Formats

Forms and formats should be uniquely designed for gathering the actual information.

Quality plan should contain the system for assurance of 'Right service to the Right user at the Right time'. It consists of a table where performance and characteristic of product, frequency of check, method of check and troubleshooting elements are tabulated. For example, a table can be generated which can check performance of service, frequency of check, method of check trouble shooting at occurrence of any fault.

Contract Review

a. The supplier shall establish and maintain documented procedures for contract review.

b. The supplier shall identify how an amendment to a contract should be made.

c. Records of contract reviews shall be maintained.

Recommendations

1. Users are the customers for the library.
2. The contract between library and users is basically defined by the library. If there is variety of users than different contracts can be made. Within a library, there are faculties, project assistants, students, staffs etc. Different contracts can be established with different kind of library users which

should be decided by the Library Management Committee. In these contracts entitlement with respect to the number of books and journals borrowed and period of borrowing can be decided.

3. These conditions should be reviewed time to time by Management Review Committee. The contract between the library and the user should be signed by both the parties. This can be done at the Request form submitted by the user.
4. Any contractual change must be communicated to user personally.

Document and Data Control

a. The supplier should establish and maintain documented procedures to control all documents and data that relate to the quality system requirements.
b. All quality documents and data should be approved and issued by competent authority.
c. Any change in the document and data should be done by competent authority and wherever it is possible mention the change from the previous one.

Recommendations

1. The type of the documents envisaged for library set up are:
   i. Quality Assurance Manual,
   ii. Quality System Procedure,
   iii. Work instructions,
   iv. International codes and references,
   v. Classification schemes,
   vi. Cataloguing codes,
   vii. Softwares etc.
2. A Master list should be made and it must have entry of all the documents under control. The entries should indicate:

i. Revision number of the document,
ii. Copy number (Number of copies in circulation),
iii. Location and
iv. Current status.

3. The obsolete documents should be immediately withdrawn and one copy may be kept in the archive.
4. Authority and responsibility for approval, issue and review of documents should be clearly defined and documented. Generally it is Management Representative for Quality Assurance Manual and respective section heads for Quality System Procedure and Work Instructions.
5. If the documents are stored in soft copy proper backup should be made access to it should be highly restricted.
6. The manual can be stored in the hard disk as well as hard copy depending on the choice of the organization.

Purchasing

a. The supplier shall establish and maintain documented procedures to ensure that purchased product.
b. Supplier shall evaluate sub-contractor.
c. Purchasing documents shall contain data clearly describing the product ordered.
d. Supplier should do verification of sub-contractor and if possible customer verification should be done.

Recommendations

1. Library should prepare the documented procedures for purchase like of books, journals, computer PC, software, stationary, etc. consumables.
2. A list of accepted vendor should be maintained. A vendor should be accepted when he/she qualifies

the laid quality requirements by the library. Thus accepted vendor should be identified and listed. A periodic review of all vendors should be done on the basis of their performance of the past and a report should be made. One copy of the report should also send to vendor. In case if a vendor is continuously failing to fulfill quality requirements should be black listed.

3. The Purchase document should have all the necessary specifications including type, grade, design and identification of the product. For example, Acquisition Section should make a Purchase document on a fixed format referred in ISO 9002. Section -in-charge or any other authority so designated should review the purchase document before sending it.
4. Library should maintain procedure for verifying purchased books or other articles at the vendor's premises if necessary. For example, in case the purchase of furniture or the computer articles for the library, Library should conduct an audit at the vender's place and check the suitability of product and its performance.
5. For the approval of books if it is possible Library can take the users to the vender's place and can get the approval by the users. For example, in the academic library or specialized library it is possible to get the approval for the books by the users by taking the users to the vendor's place.

Control of Customer-supplied Product

Organization should document and control the customer's supplied product

Recommendations

1. In the library examples of customer supplied products are:

a. Reader's ticket,

b. Customer query and

c. Reference query

2. It should be clearly documented how to handle these items. For example, how the cards should be processed and protected from any damage or lost during the time it is their custody.
3. Any nonconformity found in such a product should be recorded and immediately brought into the notice of user. For example, if the query asked is not correct it should be informed to the user.

Product identification and traceability

Each and every product in the library should be identified in the library.

Recommendations

1. None of the article including books, journals, PCs, etc. in the library should remain unidentified. For example, if a lot of books enter in the library or any other sort of product or material enters in the library, should be identified at once. Any information of user provision or library use should be uniquely identified.
2. For this unique identification mark or number can be given to such entities.
3. All capital item used in the library procedures also should be uniquely identified.

Process Control

The supplier shall prepare documented procedure and plan for production, installation and servicing which directly affects.

Recommendations

1. Library should define each of these process in its Procedure Manual:

   i. Acquisition section,
   ii. Maintenance section,
   iii. Reference section,
   iv. Reprography section,
   v. Circulation section,
   vi. Administration section,
   vii. Technical section,
   viii. Journal procurement section, etc.

2. Processes should be approved by In-charge of the section.
3. Process should be defined in the written statements or in the form of flow-charts which, brings more clarity.
4. In the definition of the processes the procedures for monitoring the process should also be included.
5. Library management should provide healthy working environment like dust-free environment and by installing instruments like ladder, shock-busters etc.
6. Periodic maintenance of equipments like Xerox machine, Vacuum cleaner, binding machines should be planned.

Inspection and Testing

a. The supplier shall establish and maintain documented procedures for inspection and testing.
b. The supplier shall ensure that incoming product is not used or processed until it has been inspected.
c. In process inspection and testing should be done.
d. Final inspection and testing should be done before delivery of product.
e. All the inspection records should be maintained.

Recommendations

1. The library should establish a format for the inspection of each individual service. For example, after technical processing of books, there should be an established procedure to check the processing.
2. Received materials whether it is books, journals or any other article should be inspected before the further processing. It should be done according to the contract made between the library and its vendor. Products should also be inspected during the process at different stages.
3. If in any case there is an urgent need for the material, received material can be used without any inspection and test but such material should be specially identified and recorded. For example, if a book is in urgent demand, it can be issued to the user but it should be specifically identified and recorded.
4. Periodical review of vendors should be done according to the performance of the vendor. Report should be generated by review. If possible, particularly in the case of articles like furniture or personal computers, library should go to the premises of vendor to inspect the laid quality standards of the library.
5. Reports should be generated out of the different levels of inspection. All the reports should be submitted at the time of final inspection of product. Submission of the reports should be checked according to quality plan.
6. Only the inspected services should be delivered to the user.
7. Reports should be recorded irrespective to the service conformance and non-conformance. The name of the inspecting authority must be mentioned on the report.

Control of Inspection, Measuring and Test Equipment

The supplier shall establish and maintain documented procedures to control, calibrate and maintain inspection, measuring and test equipment.

Recommendations

1. Library should calibrate its Burglar alarm, Xeroxing machine counter, system software, digitization machine, etc. These equipments should be calibrated periodically.
2. The source of calibration should traceable to national/international standards.
3. Records of calibration should be kept.

Inspection and test status

The inspection and test status of product shall be identified by suitable means, which indicates the conformance of product with regard to inspection and test performed.

Recommendations

Library should develop a procedure which states the status of books/journals processing. For example, it should state the status as:

- Waiting for accession,
- Waiting for binding or
- Waiting for disposal etc.

Control of nonconforming products

The supplier shall establish and maintain documented procedures to ensure conformity of product. Nonconforming product should be reviewed in accordance with documented procedures.

Recommendations

1. Any nonconformity occurred in services or any complaint about service should be identified and recorded.

2. Nonconforming product should be analyzed (or trouble-shoot) on quarterly basis.

Corrective and preventive action

The supplier shall establish and maintain documented procedures for implementing corrective and preventive action.

Recommendations

1. The nonconformity or complaint should be recorded and analyzed.
2. Corrective & preventive actions should be identified and implemented.
3. Validity of corrective and preventive actions should be reviewed by way of trial implementation and audit follow-up.
4. The result should be documented.

Handling, storage, packaging, preservation and delivery

Supplier should identify proper handling, storage, packaging, preservation and delivery.

Recommendations

1. Library should define the procedure for handling the library materials like, CD-ROMs, Magnetic Tapes, manuscripts. Process for the same should be exhibited at the key places in the library, to bring awareness on safe handling.
2. Standard temperature and pressure should be maintained according to the product.
3. All the staff should be made aware of safety measures in the library.
4. Periodically, insecticides should be administered on the stack of books.
5. Secure packaging should be done while transportation. For example, Inter-library loan.

6. Libraries housekeeping job should be equally imparted to the staff and strictly maintained.

Control of quality records

The supplier shall establish and maintain documented procedures for identification, collection, indexing, access, filing, storage, maintenance and disposition of quality records.

Recommendations

1. The quality records must be stored, indexed and filed in such a way that their retrieval become easy whenever it is needed.
2. Records should be stored at appropriate place and in the suitable conditions.
3. For each record a retention time should be maintained and strictly adhered to.
4. Records can be stored in electronic format also.
5. Library should define how to dispose records after the retention period.

Internal quality audit

The supplier shall establish and maintain documented procedures for planning and implementing internal quality audits to verify quality activities.

Recommendations

1. Library should conduct Internal Quality Audits.
2. The objective of audit is to check the performance of the library services. The objective of the audit should be clearly communicated in the library.
3. Audit should be carried out at different intervals and the frequency must be determined according to the importance of the work.
4. The members of the team should be trained to conduct internal audit.

5. An auditor cannot audit its own department. For example, an auditor belonging to Technical Section cannot audit Technical Section.
6. The procedure to conduct internal audits must be documented.
7. Findings of such audit must be recorded and presented in the form of report to Management review.

Training

The supplier shall establish and maintain documented procedures for identifying training needs and provision of training.

Recommendations

1. The need for training should be identified. The situation for training can be:
   i. When it is found that the certain process is performed unsatisfactorily due to inadequate knowledge.
   ii. Introduction of new technology or equipment.
2. Library should work to upgrade skills of employees. It should conduct time to time seminars, workshop or training programs for upgrading.
3. Records of such training should be kept and feedback from the training provision should be reviewed and effectiveness should be measured in the library.

Servicing

Where servicing is a specified requirement, the supplier shall establish and maintain documented procedure for performing, verifying and reporting that the servicing meets the specified requirements.

Recommendation

This clause is not applicable in the library.

Statistical techniques

a. The supplier shall identify the need for statistical techniques.

b. The supplier shall establish and maintain documented procedures to implement and control the application of the statistical techniques.

Recommendations

1. Q7 tools and other statistical quality control techniques such as: S. P. C., Sampling plans, Sample survey techniques, User survey techniques, Estimation, Test of Hypothesis, ANOVA etc. are generally applicable to the analysis and improvement in the library resources & services.
2. A procedure manual elaborating the techniques to use simplement in improving Library sources and services should be prepared and awareness should be provided.

EXERCISES

1. Discuss the role of five laws of library science in establishing a library quality system.
2. Discuss Management Responsibility in the successful implementation of Quality System.
3. What are different levels of documentation that can be done in a library.
4. How can document control be done in the library?
5. What procedure should be followed by a library to establish their purchase policy.
6. Discuss the importance of internal audit control in context to libraries.
7. Explain the importance of training of the library staff can improve the quality of library services.

7
Conclusion

It goes without saying that 'Quality in Service' has caught the imagination of the world in the last decade. Service providers have to face the new challenges if TQM in the service sector is to become a reality.

Many a service provider e.g. Hospitals, Builders, Educational institutions etc have already begin the journey towards TQM by working for ISO 9001/9002 certification. It is needless to say that ISO 9000 accreditation is only the beginning of the journey towards excellence in whatever we do. At the same time focus should not be merely on obtaining the certificate, but bringing values to the organization through the implementation of ISO 9000 series Q. M. S. (Quality Management System).

Value added opportunities have been provided in the ISO 9000 standards, in almost every clause/ requirement. For example:

	Clause(s) of ISO 9002	*Scope of value addition by activities*
4.1	Management review	Management review
4.2	Quality planning	Quality planning
4.3	Contract review	Contract review

4.5	Purchasing	Vendor evaluation and feedback
4.9	Inspection and testing	Calibration control
4.13	Corrective actions	Corrective and preventive actions
4.16	Internal quality audit	Internal quality audit
4.17	Training	Training

The organizations have to adapt the system laid down in 'letter and spirit'.

As far as the libraries are concerned, there exists no exception for them. User expectations are the standards upon which the performance of the libraries should be judged. Information needs of the users are dynamic, so is the services expected and demanded by them. Libraries need to evolve themselves with the changing expectations and work towards the development of new service models, proving their indispensable role in the educational process. Strategies to be adopted may include timely review of existing services, appraisal of internal quality audit findings, devising new service models and revising or remodeling it on the basis of user feedback. ISO 9000 provides the guidelines to "measure the services" offered by the library.

"Total quality management is a journey, not a destination." ~Berry. So, lets start the journey.

References

1. Adesola, Akinyele. Total Quality Management. Centre for Industrial Research and Development.
2. Al-Zamany, Y., Hoddell, E.J. and Savage, B.M. (2002). "Understanding the difficulties of implementing quality management in Yemen", The TQM Magazine, Vol. 14 No. 4, pp. 240-7.
3. American Society for Quality. Quality Glossary. Available at *http://asq.org/glossary/q.html* (accessed on 8/5/2015)
4. Angel R. Martínez Lorente, Frank Dewhurst, Barrie G. Dale, (1998) "Total quality management: origins and evolution of the term", The TQM Magazine, Vol. 10 Iss: 5, pp.378 - 386
5. Applying ISO 9000 quality management system, ITC: Geneva, 1996, 139 p.
6. Bartlett, C.A. and Ghoshal, S. (1992). Transnational Management: Text, Cases and Readings in Cross-border Management. Homewood, IL:Irwin.
7. Besterfied, D. H. (1990). Quality control. Prentice Hall.
8. Butcher, K. S. (1993). Total quality management: The Oregon State University Library's experience. "Journal of Library Administration," 18(1/2), 45-56. (EJ 469 102)

9. Caplan, R. H. (1988). Practical Approach to Quality Control. Business Books.

10. Central Library, IIT Madras. ISO 9001. Available at *http://www.cenlib.iitm.ac.in/docs/library/index.php?page=iso9001* (accessed on 6/4/2015)

11. Cochran, C. (2008). ISO 9001 in Plain English. Paton Professional. 178 p.

12. Cook, Colleen and Heath, Fred M. (2001). Users' Perceptions of Library Service Quality: A LibQUAL+ Qualitative Study. Library Trends, Vol. 49 (4), pp. 548-584. Available at http://www.libqual.org/documents/admin/cookheath.pdf (Retrieved on 2.4.2015)

13. Crosby, P.B. (1984). Quality without tears: The Art of Hassle-Free Management. McGraw-Hill: New York. 205 p.

14. Crosby, Philip (1995). Quality Is Still Free: Making Quality Certain in Uncertain Times. 2nd Ed. McGraw-Hill.

15. Deming, W. Edward, Out of the crisis: quality productivity and competitive position, Productivity and Quality: Madras, 1986, 507 p..

16. Deming, W.E. (1986). Out of the Crisis, MIT, Centre for Advanced Engineering, Cambridge, MA.

17. Düren, Petra (2012). Total Quality Management in Academic Libraries – Best Practices. Qualitative and Quantitative Methods in Libraries (QQML). pp. 43-50. Available at http://www.qqml.net/papers/July_Issue/5QQML_Journal_2012_Duren_1_43-50.pdf (accessed on 2/4/2015)

18. Ellis, Debbie and Norton, Bob, Implementing BS 5750/ ISO 9000 in libraries, Aslib: London, 1993, 123 p.

19. Elmuti, Dean and Kathawala, Yunus (1997). An overview of benchmarking process: a tool for

continuous improvement and competitive advantage. Benchmarking for Quality Management & Technology, Vol. 4(4), pp. 229-243. Available at http://consensus.liu.se/cng/wp-content/uploads/2010/04/Benchmarking.pdf (accessed on 5.4.2015)

20. Evans, James R. and Lindsay, William M. (2010). Managing for Quality and Performance Excellence. 8th edition. South-Western. pp. 61.

21. Faisal Talib, Zillur Rahman, M.N. Qureshi, (2011). "Analysis of interaction among the barriers to total quality management implementation using interpretive structural modeling approach", Benchmarking: An International Journal, Vol. 18 Iss: 4, pp.563 – 587.

22. Feigenbaum, A. V., Total quality control, 3rd Rev. ed. McGraw-Hill: New York, 1991, pp. 1-26.

23. George, S. (1998). Total Quality Management: Strategies and Techniques Proven at Today's Most Successful Companies. 2nd ed. Wiley. 254 p.

24. Goetsch, David L. and Davis, Stanley B (1997). Quality Management. 2nd ed. Prentice-Hall: New Jersey, pp. 1-33.

25. Goldratt, Eliyahu M. and Cox, Jeff. (1993). The Goal. 2nd ed. Productivity: Madras, 335 p.

26. Grant, E. L. and R. S. Leavenworth (1988). Statistical Quality Control. McGraw-Hill: New York.

27. Hackman, J.R. and Wageman, R. (1995, "Total quality management: empirical, conceptual, and practical issues", Administrative Science Quarterly, Vol. 40 No. 2, pp. 309 42

28. Halkar, G. and K. Govindrajulu (2014). TQM in Libraries: Challenges To Stimulate Change. Asian Journal of Multidisciplinary Studies. Vol. 2 (1). Available at www.ajms.co.in (accessed on 3/1/2015)

29. Hansson, J., Backlund, Fredrik and Lycke, Liselott

(2003). "Managing commitment: increasing the odds for successful implementation of TQM, TPM or RCM", International Journal of Quality & Reliability Management, Vol. 20 (9), pp.993 - 1008.

30. Harvey, L., 2004–14, Analytic Quality Glossary. Quality Research International. Available at *http://www.qualityresearchinternational.com/glossary/*

31. Hauser, J.R. and Clausing, D. (1988, "The house of quality", Harvard Business Review, Vol. 66 No. 3, pp. 63 73.

32. Hoyle, D. (2007). Quality Management Essentials. Routledge. 224 p.

33. Ijirigho, Mercy A. (2010). Faculty Expectations of Libraries: A Comparative Study of Covenant University and the University of Lagos. Library Philosophy and Practice. Available at http://digitalcommons.unl.edu/cgi/viewcontent.cgi?article=1318&context=libphilprac (Retrieved on 20.4.2015)

34. International Organization for Standardization (2012). Quality Management Principles. Available at http://www.iso.org/iso/qmp_2012.pdf (accessed on 6/12/2014)

35. International Organization for Standardization Homepage, *http://www.iso.ch/*

36. Ishikawa, K, What is total quality control? The japanese way, Prentice-Hall: London,1985, 215p.

37. Ishikawa, K. (1985). What is Total Quality Control? The Japanese Way.

38. ISO 9000 quality management system : guidelines for enterprises in developing countries, 2nd ed., ITC : Geneva, 1996, 319 p.

39. ISO standards compendium: ISO 9000 quality management system, 5th ed. ISO : Geneva, 374 p.

40. J. M. Juran, The quality triology, *Quality Progress*, Aug. 1986.

41. Juran, J. M. (1967). "The QC Circle Phenomenon," Industrial Quality Control, January 1967, pp. 329-36.

42. Juran, J. M. (1986). The Quality Trilogy: A Universal Approach to Managing for Quality. In ASQC 40th Annual Quality Congress in Anaheim, California, May 20, 1986.

43. Juran, J. M. (1992). Juran on Quality by Design: The New Steps for Planning Quality into Goods and Services. Revised. Simon and Schuster. 538 p.

44. Jurow, S. & Barnard, S. B. (1993). Introduction: TQM fundamentals and overview of contents. "Journal of Library Administration," 18(1/2), 1-13. (EJ 469 099)

45. Kemp, S. (2005). Quality Management Demystified. McGraw-Hill. 320 p.

46. Lampercht, James L. (1992). ISO 9000: Preparing for Registration. ASQC: New York. 241p.

47. Leavengood, S. and Reeb, J. (1999). How and Why SPC Works. Available at http://ir.library.oregonstate.edu/xmlui/bitstream/handle/1957/20085/em8733-e.pdf (accessed on 1.4.2015)

48. Malhotra, S. (2006). Quality Management: Awareness, Planning, Control and Improvement in the Global Economy. Deep and Deep Publications. 304 p.

49. Manikandan.G (2005). Total Quality Management. Available at http://tqmnotes.blogspot.in/ (accessed on 12/4/2016)

50. Martínez-Lorente, Angel R. and Martínez-Costa, Micaela. ISO 9000 & TQM: Substitutes or Complementaries? An Empirical Study in Industrial Companies. Available at http://www.researchgate.

net/profile/Angel_Martinez-Lorente/publication/235253953 _ ISO_9000_and_TQM_substitutes_or_complementaries_ An_empirical_ study_ in_industrial_companies/links/004635208b09b6c44a000000.pdf (accessed on 30.4.2015)

51. Masters, Denise G. (1997). Total Quality Management in Libraries. ERIC Digest. Available at http://www.ericdigests.org/1997-1/tqm.html (accessed on 2/4/2015)

52. Milakovich, M.E. (1991, "Total quality management in the public sector", National Productivity Review, Vol. 10 No. 2, pp. 195 213.

53. Miller, R.G. and Stearns, B. (1994). "Quality management for today's academic library", College & Research Libraries News, Vol. 55 (7), pp. 406-22.

54. Moghaddam, Golnessa Galyani and Moballeghi. Total Quality Management in Library and Information Sectors. Available at http://core.ac.uk/download/pdf/11885486.pdf (accessed on 30/4/2015)

55. Mola, Núria Balagué (2007). The use of ISO 9001 quality standard in higher education institution libraries. Available at *http://bid.ub.edu/19balag3.htm* (accessed on 8/4/2015)

56. Montgomery, D.C. (1997). Introduction to Statistical Quality Control, 3rd ed. New York: John Wiley & Sons. 677 pp.

57. Nameer (2009). Total Quality Management. Available at *https://totalqualitymanagement.wordpress.com/2009/02/25/deming-cycle-the-wheel-of-continuous-improvement/* (accessed on 5.4.2015)

58. Oakland, J. S. (1991). "One Way to Delight Your Customers". Works Management, Vol. 43 No. 5, pp. 65-71.

59. Pyzdek, Thomas and Keller, Paul (2012). The

Handbook for Quality Management, Second Edition: A Complete Guide to Operational Excellence. 2nd ed. McGraw-Hill.

60. Rago, W.V. (1994, "Adapting total quality management (TQM) to government: another point of view", Public Administration Review, Vol. 54 No. 1, pp. 61 4.

61. Saroja, G and Sujatha, G. Application of Total Quality Management to Library and Information Services in Indian Open Universities. Available at *http://www.col.org/forum/PCFpapers/saroja.pdf* (accessed on 3/4/2015)

62. Schmidt, W. and Finnigan, J. (1993). TQManager: A Practical Guide for Managing in a Total Quality Organization. San Francisco: Jossey-Bass Inc.

63. Schneider, B., Brief, A.P. and Guzzo, R.A. (1996). "Creating a climate and culture for sustainable organizational change", Organizational Dynamics, Vol. 24, pp. 7-19.

64. Sephari, Mehran, *ed.* Quest for quality: managing the total quality system, Industrial engineering and Management Press : Georgia, 1987, pp. 25-59.

65. Shin, D., Kalinowski, J.G. and El-Enein, G.A. (1998). "Critical implementation issues in total quality management", SAM Advanced Management Journal, Vol. 63, pp. 10-15.

66. Sohal, A.S., Samson, D. and Ramsay, L. (1998). "Requirement for successful implementation of total quality management", International Journal of Technology Management, Vol. 16, pp. 505-19.

67. Sokoviæ, M., et.al. (2009). Basic Quality Tools in Continuous Improvement Process. Strojniški vestnik - Journal of Mechanical Engineering. Vol. 55(5). Available at *http://lab.fs.uni-lj.si/labod/documents/2014/ZK/ZK14%20Dodatno%20gradivo.pdf* (accessed on 1.4.2015)

68. Taguchi, G. (1989). Quality Engineering in Production Systems. McGraw-Hill: New York.

69. Taguchi, Genichi (1987). System of experimental design: engineering methods to optimize quality and minimize costs. Vol. 2, Kraus: New York. 1189 p.

70. Tata, J., Prasad, S. and Thorn, R. (1999). "The influence of organizational structure on the effectiveness of TQM programs", Journal of Managerial Issues, Vol. 11, pp. 440-53.

71. Thessaloniki (2006). Kaizen Definition & Principles: In Brief, a Concept & Tool for Employees Involvement. Available at: http://www.michailolidis.gr/pdf/KAIZEN08.pdf (accessed on 13/9/2014)

72. Todd, J. K. (2006). On Track to Quality. Lighthouse Point Press. 144p.

73. Total Quality Management. Available at http://fkm.utm.my/~shari/download/qc02%20total%20quality%20management.pdf (accessed on 30/4/2015)

74. Townsend, P. L. and Gebhardt, Joan E. (1999). Quality is Everybody's Business. CRC Press. 392 p.

75. Trompenaars, F. (1994). Riding the Waves of Culture. New York: Irwin.

76. Udupa, S.R. (1986). "Quality Circles, Progress through Participation". New Delhi: McGraw-Hill.

77. Vlasceanu, L., Grunberg, L. and Parlea, D. (2007). Quality Assurance and Accreditation: A Glossary of Basic Terms and Definitions. Available at *http://unesdoc.unesco.org/images/0013/001346/134621e.pdf* (accessed on 1/3/2015)

78. Webber, L. and Wallace, M. (2012). Quality Control for Dummies. 384 p.

79. Wilkinson, A., Redman, T. and Shape, E. (1995).

"New patterns of quality management in the United Kingdom", Quality Management Journal, Vol. 2(2), pp. 37-51.

80. Work Group for Community Health and Development (2014). Achieving and Maintaining Quality Performance. Available at http://ctb.ku.edu/en/table-of-contents/maintain/maintain-quality-performance/overview/main (accessed on 1.4.2015)

Glossary

ACCREDITATION : It is the establishment of the status, legitimacy or appropriateness of an institution, programme or module of study.

AUDIT : Audit, in the context of quality in higher education, is a process for checking that procedures are in place to assure quality, integrity or standards of provision and outcomes.

AUSPICES : Auspices is the provenance under which a quality monitoring agency (or other evaluation body) operates.

PROVISION : Provision is an all-encompassing term that refers to the learning opportunities, research and community activity offered/undertaken by an institution of higher education.

BENCHMARK : A standard, a reference point, or a criterion against which the quality of something can be measured, judged, and evaluated, and against which outcomes of a specified activity can be measured. The term, benchmark, means a measure of best practice performance. The existence of a benchmark is one necessary step in the overall process of benchmarking.

BENCHMARKING : A standardized method for collecting and reporting critical operational data in a way that enables relevant comparisons among the performances of different organizations or programmes, usually with a view to establishing good practice, diagnosing problems in performance, and identifying areas of strength. Benchmarking gives the organization (or the programme) the external references and the best practices on which to base its evaluation and to design its working processes. It is a self-improvement and diagnostic instrument.

BEST PRACTICE : A method or an innovative process involving a range of safe and reasonable practices resulting in the improved performance of a higher education institution or programme, usually recognized as "best" by other peer organizations. A best practice does not necessarily represent an absolute, ultimate example or pattern, its application assures the improved performance of a higher education institution or programme; rather, it identifies the best approach to a specific situation, as institutions and programmes vary greatly in constituencies and scope.

CAUSE AND EFFECT DIAGRAM : A tool for analyzing process dispersion. It is also referred to as the "Ishikawa diagram," because Kaoru Ishikawa developed it, and the "fishbone diagram," because the complete diagram resembles a fish skeleton. The diagram illustrates the main causes and subcauses leading to an effect (symptom). The cause and effect diagram is one of the "seven tools of quality" (see listing).

CERTIFICATION : The process by which an agency or an association acknowledges the achievement of established quality standards and usually grants certain privileges to the target individual (student or teacher).

PROTOCOL : Detailed instructions describing planning,

control and presenting the results of research.

QUALITY : Quality in higher education is a multi-dimensional, multilevel, and dynamic concept that relates to the contextual settings of an educational model, to the institutional mission and objectives, as well as to specific standards within a given system, institution, programme, or discipline. Quality may thus take different, sometimes conflicting, meanings depending on (i) the understanding of various interests of different constituencies or stakeholders in higher education (e.g. students; universities; disciplines; the labour market; society; a government); (ii) its references: inputs, processes, outputs, missions, objectives, etc.; (iii) the attributes or characteristics of the academic world worth evaluating; and(iv) the historical period in the development of higher education.

QUALITY ASSESSMENT/ REVIEW : The actual process of external evaluation (reviewing, measuring, judging) of the quality of an organization's processes, practices, programmes, and services.

QUALITY AUDIT : A systematic, independent examination and review to determine whether quality activities and related results comply with plans and whether these plans are implemented effectively and are suitable to achieve the objectives.

QUALITY CIRCLE : A quality improvement or self-improvement study group composed of a small number of employees (10 or fewer) and their supervisor. Quality circles originated in Japan, where they are called quality control circles.

QUALITY MANAGEMENT : Quality management is the process, supported by policies and systems, used by an institution to maintain and enhance the quality of education experienced by its customers/

students and of the research undertaken by its staff.

QUALITY MANAGEMENT SYSTEM (QMS) : A formalized system that documents the structure, responsibilities and procedures required to achieve effective quality management. It involves a set of integrated policies and practices that structure the management, implementation and adaptation of quality assurance processes.

QUALITY PLAN : A document or set of documents that describe the standards, quality practices, resources and processes pertinent to a specific product, service or project.

QUALITY POLICY : An organization's general statement of its beliefs about quality, how quality will come about and its expected result.

QUALITY TRILOGY : A three-pronged approach to managing for quality. The three legs are quality planning (developing the products and processes required to meet customer needs), quality control (meeting product and process goals) and quality improvement (achieving unprecedented levels of performance).

Question Bank

1. Define Quality. Why it is required?
2. Give an historical account of the evolution of the concept "Quality".
3. What is TQM?
4. How do Quality Control and Quality Assurance differ?
5. Explain the importance of customer satisfaction.
6. Compare Juran's and Deming's approach to Quality.
7. State underlying principles of TQM.
8. Explain Juran Trilogy.
9. What is Benchmarking?
10. Enumerate Deming's 14 points of philosophy of management?
11. What are barriers to TQM implementation?
12. Explain
    - PDSA Cycle
    - Quality Circle
    - Six Sigma
    - Quality tools
    - What is ISO?
    - What is ISO 9000?
    - What are the standards in ISO 9000 family of standards?

13. What does ISO mean?
    a. International Standards Organization
    b. Internal Organization for Standardization
    c. International Organization of Standards
    d. International Organization for Standardization
14. What does ISO do?
    a. Provides organizations with information about quality management systems
    b. Helps organizations become certified under the international standard
    c. Government responsibilities and tasks in various countries
    d. Both a and b
15. Quality management is
    a. Productivity and efficiency
    b. Providing easily accessible documentation for procedures and work instructions
    c. Improving the quality of the end product or service
    d. All of the above
16. What does an audit do?
    a. Provides data for management to use in evaluating quality management policies and procedures
    b. Provides an accurate picture of conformance to the ISO standard
    c. Gives management personal information about staff members
    d. Attempts to track exactly what the staff do all day at their jobs
17. Working together for excellence is
    a. Top management work

b. Team work

c. Employee work

d. None of the above

18. ISO is based on

e. Plan, do, Check, Act

f. Employee satisfaction

g. Employee participation

h. None of the above

19. Match the following: -

1. Juran	i. Quality is the loss that a product costs to society after being shipped other than any loser by its intrinsic functions
2. Crosby	ii. Total Quality Control
3. Taguchi	iii. Quality is conformance to requirements or specifications
4. Feigenabaum	iv. Quality is fitness for use

Code

a. 1-iv, 2-iii, 3-i, 4-ii

b. 1-ii, 2-iii, 3-iv, 4-i

c. 1-i, 2-ii, 3-iii, 4-iv

d. None of the above **Ans. (a)**

20. Quality is _______ and ________.

a. Customer satisfaction, fitness for use.

b. Fitness for use, prominence of product quality

c. Conformance to specifications, customers satisfaction

d. External customer satisfaction, Internal customer satisfaction

Ans. (a)

21. A ________ is anyone who is impacted by the product or process.
    a. Buyer
    b. Customer
    c. Seller
    d. Consumer **Ans. (b)**
22. Quality is ______ to customer satisfaction
    a. Relative
    b. Productive
    c. Excellence
    d. Requirement **Ans. (a)**
23. Quality is –
    a. Relative
    b. Degree of excellence
    c. Cardinal priority of the organizations
    d. All of the above **Ans. (d)**
24. Increasing the quality of design leads to –
    a. Higher conformance
    b. Higher costs
    c. Lower cost
    d. All of the above **Ans. (b)**
25. ________ refers to quality of conformance.
    a. Higher conformance
    b. Freedom from deficiencies
    c. Customer satisfaction
    d. Fewer complaints **Ans. (b)**
26. ________ and ________ are the main determinants of satisfaction.
    a. Internal customer satisfaction, External customer satisfaction
    b. Customer satisfaction, quality of conformance

c. Product features, freedom from deficiencies

d. All of the above **Ans. (c)**

27. Quality is –

a. Productive

b. Excellence

c. Relative

d. Requirement **Ans. (c)**

28. Quality depends on the ________ of a person in a given situation.

a. Dependability

b. Physical bodies

c. Perception

d. None of the above **Ans. (a)**

29. Find the correct option

1. "Little Q"	i. End user/external customer
2. "Big Q"	ii. Internal as well as external customer
	iii. Processes directly related to manufacture of goods
	iv. All industries, services, manufacturing, government etc

Code

a. 1-i, iii & 2-ii, iv

b. 1-i, ii & 2-iii, iv

c. 1-iii, iv & 2-i, ii

d. 1-iii, ii & 2-i, iv **Ans. (a)**

30. Total quality Management (TQM) is:-

a. It means meeting the requirements of the internal / external customer consistently by continuous improvement in the quality of work of all employees

b. It is the system of activities directed at achieving delighted customers, empowered employees, higher revenues & lower costs

c. It is the application of quantitative methods & human resources to improve the product services

d. All of the above **Ans. (d)**

31. It is a management philosophy, a journey to organizational excellence through customer orientation.

a. TQM

b. Quality Control

c. Quality Control & Inspection

d. Both a & b **Ans. (a)**

32. Customer is concerned with –

a. Quality

b. Cost

c. Delivery

d. All of the above **Ans. (d)**